# THE DEFORMED TRANSFORMED: A DRAMA

Written by
Lord Byron

Edited by
Ernest Hartley Coleridge

2015

# Table of Contents

# INTRODUCTION TO THE DEFORMED TRANSFORMED.

THE date of the original MS. of The Deformed Transformed is "Pisa, 1822." There is nothing to show in what month it was written, but it may be conjectured that it was begun and finished within the period which elapsed between the death of Allegra, April 20, and the death of Shelley, July 8, 1822. According to Medwin (Conversations, 1824, p. 227), an unfavourable criticism of Shelley's ("It is a bad imitation of Faust"), together with a discovery that "two entire lines" of Southey's—

"And water shall see thee,

And fear thee, and flee thee"—

were imbedded in one of his "Songs," touched Byron so deeply that he "threw the poem into the fire," and concealed the existence of a second copy for more than two years. It is a fact that Byron's correspondence does not contain the remotest allusion to The Deformed Transformed; but, with regard to the plagiarism from Southey, in the play as written in 1822 there is neither Song nor Incantation which could have contained two lines from The Curse of Kehama.

As a dramatist, Byron's function, or métier, was twofold. In Manfred, in Cain, in Heaven and Earth, he is concerned with the analysis and evolution of metaphysical or ethical notions; in Marino Faliero, in Sardanapalus, and The Two Foscari, he set himself "to dramatize striking passages of history;" in The Deformed Transformed he sought to combine the solution of a metaphysical puzzle or problem, the relation of personality to individuality, with the scenic rendering of a striking historical episode, the Sack of Rome in 1527.

In the note or advertisement prefixed to the drama, Byron acknowledges that "the production" is founded partly on the story of a forgotten novel, The Three Brothers, and partly on "the Faust of the great Goethe."[470]

Arnaud, or Julian, the hero of The Three Brothers (by Joshua Pickersgill, jun., 4 vols., 1803), "sells his soul to the Devil, and becomes an arch-fiend in order to avenge himself for the taunts of strangers on the deformity of his person" (see Gent. Mag., November, 1804, vol. 74, p. 1047; and post, pp. 473-479). The idea of an escape from natural bonds or disabilities by supernatural means and at the price of the soul or will, the un-Christlike surrender to the tempter, which is the grund-stoff of the Faust-legend, was brought home to Byron, in the first instance, not by Goethe, or Calderon, or Marlowe, but by Joshua Pickersgill. A fellow-feeling lent an intimate and peculiar interest to the theme. He had suffered all his life from a painful and inconvenient defect, which his proud and sensitive spirit had magnified into a deformity. He had been stung to the quick by his mother's taunts and his sweetheart's ridicule, by the jeers of the base and thoughtless, by slanderous and brutal paragraphs in newspapers. He could not forget that he was lame. If his enemies had but possessed the wit, they might have given him "the sobriquet of Le Diable Boiteux" (letter to Moore, April 2, 1823, Letters, 1901, vi. 179). It was no wonder that so poignant, so persistent a calamity should be "reproduced in his poetry" (Life, p. 13), or that his passionate impatience of such a "thorn in the flesh" should picture to itself a mysterious and unhallowed miracle of healing. It is true, as Moore says (Life, pp. 45, 306), that "the trifling deformity of his foot" was the embittering circumstance of his life, that it "haunted him like a curse;" but it by no means follows that he seriously regarded his physical peculiarity as a stamp of the Divine reprobation, that "he was possessed by an idée fixe that every blessing would be 'turned into a curse' to him" (letter of Lady Byron to H. C. Robinson,

Diary, etc., 1869, in. 435, 436). No doubt he indulged himself in morbid fancies, played with the extravagances of a restless imagination, and wedded them to verse; but his intellect, "brooding like the day, a master o'er a slave," kept guard. He would never have pleaded on his own behalf that the tyranny of an idée fixe, a delusion that he was predestined to evil, was an excuse for his short-comings or his sins.

Byron's very considerable obligations to The Three Brothers might have escaped notice, but the resemblance between his "Stranger," or "Cæsar," and the Mephistopheles of "the great Goethe" was open and palpable.

If Medwin may be trusted (Conversations, 1824, p. 210), Byron had read "Faust in a sorry French translation," and it is probable that Shelley's inspired rendering of "May-day[471] Night," which was published in The Liberal (No. i., October 14, 1822, pp. 123-137), had been read to him, and had attracted his attention. The Deformed Transformed is "a Faustish kind of drama;" and Goethe, who maintained that Byron's play as a whole was "no imitation," but "new and original, close, genuine, and spirited," could not fail to perceive that "his devil was suggested by my Mephistopheles" (Conversations, 1874, p. 174). The tempter who cannot resist the temptation of sneering at his own wiles, who mocks for mocking's sake, is not Byron's creation, but Goethe's. Lucifer talked at the clergy, if he did not "talk like a clergyman;" but the "bitter hunchback," even when he is solus, sneers as the river wanders, "at his own sweet will." He is not a doctor, but a spirit of unbelief!

The second part of The Deformed Transformed represents, in three scenes, the Siege and Sack of Rome in 1527. Byron had read Robertson's Charles the Fifth (ed. 1798, ii. 313-329) in his boyhood (Life, p. 47), but it is on record that he had studied, more or less closely, the narratives of contemporary authorities. A note to The Prophecy of Dante (Poetical Works, 1901, iv. 258) refers to the Sacco di Roma, descritto da Luigi

Guicciardini, and the Ragguaglio Storico ... sacco di Roma dell' anno MDXXVII. of Jacopo Buonaparte; and it is evident that he was familiar with Cellini's story of the marvellous gests and exploits quorum maxima pars fuit, which were wrought at "the walls by the Campo Santo," or on the ramparts of the Castle of San Angelo.

The Sack of Rome was a great national calamity, and it was something more: it was a profanation and a sacrilege. The literature which it evoked was a cry of anguish, a prophetic burden of despair. "Chants populaires," writes M. Emile Gebhart (De l'Italie, "Le Sac de Rome en 1527," 1876, pp. 267,sq.), "Nouvelles de Giraldi Cintio, en forme de Décaméron ... récits historiques ... de César Grollier, Dialogues anonymes ... poésies de Pasquin, toute une littérature se developpa sur ce thème douloureux.... Le Lamento di Roma, œuvre étrange, d'inspiration gibeline, rappelle les espérances politiques exprimées jadis par Dante ... 'Bien que César m'ait dépouille'e de liberté, nous avons toujours été d'accord dans une même volonté. Je ne me lamenterais pas si lui régnait; mais je crois qu'il est ressuscité, ou qu'il ressuscitera véritablement, car souvent un Ange m'a annoncé qu'un César viendrait me délivrer.'... Enfin, voici une chanson française que répétaient en repassant les monts les soldats du Marquis de Saluces:—

"Parlons de la déffaiete

De ces pouvres Rommains,[472]

Aussi de la complainete

De notre père saint.

"'O noble roy de France,

Regarde en pitié

L'Eglise en ballance ...

Pour Dieu! ne tarde plus,

C'est ta mère, ta substance;

O fils, n'en faictz reffus.'"

"Le dernier monument," adds M. Gebhart, in a footnote, "de cette littérature, est le singulier drame de Byron, The

Deformed Transformed, dont Jules César est le héros, et le Sac de Rome le cadre."

It is unlikely that Byron, who read everything he could lay his hands upon, and spared no trouble to master his "period," had not, either at first or second hand, acquainted himself with specimens of this popular literature. (For La Presa e Lamento di Roma, Romæ Lamentatio, etc., see Lamenti Storici dei Secoli xiv., xv. (Medin e Fratri), Scelta di Curiosità, etc., 235, 236, 237, Bologna, 1890, vol. iii. See, too, for "Chanson sur la Mort du Connétable de Bourbon," Recueil de Chants historiques français, par A. J. V. Le Roux de Lincy, 1842, ii. 99.) The Deformed Transformed was published by John Hunt, February 20, 1824. A third edition appeared February 23, 1824. It was reviewed, unfavourably, in the London Magazine, March, 1824, vol. 9, pp. 315-321; the Scots Magazine, March, 1824, N.S. vol. xiv. pp. 353-356; and in the Monthly Review, March, 1824, Enlarged Series, 103, pp. 321, 324. One reviewer, however (London Magazine), had the candour to admit that "Lord Byron may write below himself, but he can never write below us!"

For the unfinished third part, vide post, pp. 532-534.

[473]

# ADVERTISEMENT

This production is founded partly on the story of a novel called "The Three Brothers,"[201] published many [474]years ago, from which M. G. Lewis's "Wood Demon"[202] was also taken; and partly on the "Faust" of the great Goethe. The present publication[203] contains the two first Parts only, and the opening chorus of the third. The rest may perhaps appear hereafter.
[475]

[476]
DRAMATIS PERSONÆ

STRANGER, afterwards CÆSAR
ARNOLD.
BOURBON.
PHILIBERT.
CELLINI.

BERTHA.
OLIMPIA.
Spirits, Soldiers, Citizens of Rome, Priests, Peasants, etc.

[477]

# THE  DEFORMED TRANSFORMED:

# PART I.

# SCENE I —A Forest.

Enter ARNOLD and his mother BERTHA.
Bert. OUT, Hunchback!
Arn.I was born so, Mother![204]
Bert.Out,
Thou incubus! Thou nightmare! Of seven sons,[478]
The sole abortion!
Arn.Would that I had been so,
And never seen the light!
Bert.I would so, too!
But as thou hast—hence, hence—and do thy best!
That back of thine may bear its burthen; 'tis
More high, if not so broad as that of others.
Arn. It bears its burthen;—but, my heart! Will it
Sustain that which you lay upon it, Mother?
I love, or, at the least, I loved you: nothing10
Save You, in nature, can love aught like me.
You nursed me—do not kill me!
Bert.Yes—I nursed thee,
Because thou wert my first-born, and I knew not
If there would be another unlike thee,
That monstrous sport of Nature. But get hence,
And gather wood![205]
Arn.I will: but when I bring it,
Speak to me kindly. Though my brothers are
So beautiful and lusty, and as free
As the free chase they follow, do not spurn me:
Our milk has been the same.
Bert.As is the hedgehog's,20
Which sucks at midnight from the wholesome dam
Of the young bull, until the milkmaid finds
The nipple, next day, sore, and udder dry.

Call not thy brothers brethren! Call me not
Mother; for if I brought thee forth, it was
As foolish hens at times hatch vipers, by
Sitting upon strange eggs. Out, urchin, out!
 [Exit BERTHA.
Arn. (solus). Oh, mother! — — She is gone, and I must do
Her bidding; — wearily but willingly
I would fulfil it, could I only hope30
A kind word in return. What shall I do?
[ARNOLD begins to cut wood: in doing this he wounds one of
his hands.
My labour for the day is over now.
Accursed be this blood that flows so fast;[479]
For double curses will be my meed now
At home — What home? I have no home, no kin,
No kind — not made like other creatures, or
To share their sports or pleasures. Must I bleed, too,
Like them? Oh, that each drop which falls to earth
Would rise a snake to sting them, as they have stung me!
Or that the Devil, to whom they liken me,40
Would aid his likeness! If I must partake[206]
His form, why not his power? Is it because
I have not his will too? For one kind word
From her who bore me would still reconcile me
Even to this hateful aspect. Let me wash
The wound.
[ARNOLD goes to a spring, and stoops to wash his hand: he
starts back.
They are right; and Nature's mirror shows me,
What she hath made me. I will not look on it
Again, and scarce dare think on't. Hideous wretch
That I am! The very waters mock me with50
My horrid shadow — like a demon placed
Deep in the fountain to scare back the cattle
From drinking therein.[He pauses.

And shall I live on,
A burden to the earth, myself, and shame
Unto what brought me into life? Thou blood,
Which flowest so freely from a scratch, let me
Try if thou wilt not, in a fuller stream,
Pour forth my woes for ever with thyself
On earth, to which I will restore, at once,
This hateful compound of her atoms, and60
Resolve back to her elements, and take
The shape of any reptile save myself,
And make a world for myriads of new worms!
This knife! now let me prove if it will sever
This withered slip of Nature's nightshade—my
Vile form—from the creation, as it hath[480]
The green bough from the forest.
[ARNOLD places the knife in the ground, with the point
upwards.
Now 'tis set,
And I can fall upon it. Yet one glance
On the fair day, which sees no foul thing like
Myself, and the sweet sun which warmed me, but70
In vain. The birds—how joyously they sing!
So let them, for I would not be lamented:
But let their merriest notes be Arnold's knell;
The fallen leaves my monument; the murmur
Of the near fountain my sole elegy.
Now, knife, stand firmly, as I fain would fall!
[As he rushes to throw himself upon the knife, his eye is
suddenly caught by the fountain, which seems in motion.
The fountain moves without a wind: but shall
The ripple of a spring change my resolve?
No. Yet it moves again! The waters stir,
Not as with air, but by some subterrane80
And rocking Power of the internal world.
What's here? A mist! No more?—

[A cloud comes from the fountain. He stands gazing upon it: it
is dispelled, and a tall black man comes towards him.[207]
Arn.What would you? Speak!
Spirit or man?
Stran.As man is both, why not
Say both in one?
Arn.Your form is man's, and yet
You may be devil.
Stran.So many men are that
Which is so called or thought, that you may add me
To which you please, without much wrong to either.
But come: you wish to kill yourself; — pursue
Your purpose.
Arn.You have interrupted me.
Stran. What is that resolution which can e'er90[481]
Be interrupted? If I be the devil
You deem, a single moment would have made you
Mine, and for ever, by your suicide;
And yet my coming saves you.
Arn.I said not
You were the Demon, but that your approach
Was like one.
Stran.Unless you keep company
With him (and you seem scarce used to such high
Society) you can't tell how he approaches;
And for his aspect, look upon the fountain,
And then on me, and judge which of us twain100
Looks likest what the boors believe to be
Their cloven-footed terror.
Arn.Do you — dare you
To taunt me with my born deformity?
Stran. Were I to taunt a buffalo with this
Cloven foot of thine, or the swift dromedary
With thy Sublime of Humps, the animals
Would revel in the compliment. And yet

Both beings are more swift, more strong, more mighty
In action and endurance than thyself,
And all the fierce and fair of the same kind110
With thee. Thy form is natural: 'twas only
Nature's mistaken largess to bestow
The gifts which are of others upon man.
Arn. Give me the strength then of the buffalo's foot,[cw]
When he spurns high the dust, beholding his
Near enemy; or let me have the long
And patient swiftness of the desert-ship,
The helmless dromedary!—and I'll bear[cx]
Thy fiendish sarcasm with a saintly patience.
Stran. I will.
Arn. (with surprise). Thou canst?
Stran.Perhaps. Would you aught else?120
Arn. Thou mockest me.
Stran.Not I. Why should I mock
What all are mocking? That's poor sport, methinks.[482]
To talk to thee in human language (for
Thou canst not yet speak mine), the forester
Hunts not the wretched coney, but the boar,
Or wolf, or lion—leaving paltry game
To petty burghers, who leave once a year
Their walls, to fill their household cauldrons with
Such scullion prey. The meanest gibe at thee,—
Now I can mock the mightiest.[cy]
Arn.Then waste not130
Thy time on me: I seek thee not.
Stran.Your thoughts
Are not far from me. Do not send me back:
I'm not so easily recalled to do
Good service.
Arn.What wilt thou do for me?
Stran.Change
Shapes with you, if you will, since yours so irks you;

Or form you to your wish in any shape.
Arn. Oh! then you are indeed the Demon, for
Nought else would wittingly wear mine.
Stran.I'll show thee
The brightest which the world e'er bore, and give thee
Thy choice.
Arn.On what condition?
Stran.There's a question!140
An hour ago you would have given your soul
To look like other men, and now you pause
To wear the form of heroes.
Arn.No; I will not.
I must not compromise my soul.
Stran.What soul,
Worth naming so, would dwell in such a carcase?
Arn. 'Tis an aspiring one, whate'er the tenement
In which it is mislodged. But name your compact:
Must it be signed in blood?
Stran.Not in your own.
Arn. Whose blood then?
Stran.We will talk of that hereafter.
But I'll be moderate with you, for I see150
Great things within you. You shall have no bond[483]
But your own will, no contract save your deeds.
Are you content?
Arn.I take thee at thy word.
Stran.  Now then! —
[The Stranger approaches the fountain, and turns to
ARNOLD.
A little of your blood.[208]
Arn.For what?
Stran. To mingle with the magic of the waters,
And make the charm effective.
Arn. (holding out his wounded arm). Take it all.
Stran. Not now. A few drops will suffice for this.

[The Stranger takes some of ARNOLD'S blood in his hand,
and casts it into the fountain.
Shadows of Beauty!
Shadows of Power!
Rise to your duty—160
This is the hour!
Walk lovely and pliant[cz]
From the depth of this fountain,
As the cloud-shapen giant
Bestrides the Hartz Mountain.[209]
Come as ye were,
That our eyes may behold
The model in air
Of the form I will mould,
Bright as the Iris170
When ether is spanned;—
Such his desire is,[Pointing to ARNOLD.
Such my command![da]
Demons heroic—
Demons who wore
The form of the Stoic
Or sophist of yore[484]—
Or the shape of each victor—
From Macedon's boy,
To each high Roman's picture,180
Who breathed to destroy—
Shadows of Beauty!
Shadows of Power!
Up to your duty—
This is the hour!
[Various phantoms arise from the waters, and pass in
succession before the Stranger and ARNOLD.
Arn. What do I see?
Stran.The black-eyed Roman,[210] with
The eagle's beak between those eyes which ne'er

Beheld a conqueror, or looked along
The land he made not Rome's, while Rome became
His, and all theirs who heired his very name.190
Arn. The phantom's bald; my quest is beauty. Could I
Inherit but his fame with his defects!
Stran. His brow was girt with laurels more than hairs.[211]
You see his aspect—choose it, or reject.
I can but promise you his form; his fame
Must be long sought and fought for.
Arn.I will fight, too,
But not as a mock Cæsar. Let him pass:
His aspect may be fair, but suits me not.
Stran. Then you are far more difficult to please
Than Cato's sister, or than Brutus's mother,200
Or Cleopatra at sixteen[212]—an age
When love is not less in the eye than heart.
But be it so! Shadow, pass on!
 [The phantom of Julius Cæsar disappears.
Arn.And can it
Be, that the man who shook the earth is gone,[db][485]
And left no footstep?
Stran.There you err. His substance
Left graves enough, and woes enough, and fame
More than enough to track his memory;
But for his shadow—'tis no more than yours,
Except a little longer and less crooked
I' the sun. Behold another![A second phantom passes.
Arn.Who is he?210
Stran. He was the fairest and the bravest of
Athenians.[213] Look upon him well.
Arn.He is
More lovely than the last. How beautiful!
Stran. Such was the curled son of Clinias;—wouldst thou
Invest thee with his form?
Arn.Would that I had

Been born with it! But since I may choose further,
I will look further.[The shade of Alcibiades disappears.
Stran.Lo! behold again!
Arn. What! that low, swarthy, short-nosed, round-eyed satyr,
With the wide nostrils and Silenus' aspect,
The splay feet and low stature![214] I had better220
Remain that which I am.
Stran.And yet he was
The earth's perfection of all mental beauty,
And personification of all virtue.
But you reject him?
Arn.If his form could bring me
That which redeemed it — no.
Stran.I have no power
To promise that; but you may try, and find it
Easier in such a form — or in your own.[486]
Arn. No. I was not born for philosophy,
Though I have that about me which has need on't.
Let him fleet on.
Stran.Be air, thou Hemlock-drinker!230
[The shadow of Socrates disappears: another rises.
Arn. What's here? whose broad brow and whose curly beard
And manly aspect look like Hercules,[215]
Save that his jocund eye hath more of Bacchus
Than the sad purger of the infernal world,
Leaning dejected on his club of conquest,[216]
As if he knew the worthlessness of those
For whom he had fought.
Stran.It was the man who lost
The ancient world for love.
Arn.I cannot blame him,
Since I have risked my soul because I find not
That which he exchanged the earth for.
Stran.Since so far240
You seem congenial, will you wear his features?

Arn. No. As you leave me choice, I am difficult.
If but to see the heroes I should ne'er
Have seen else, on this side of the dim shore,
Whence they float back before us.
Stran.Hence, Triumvir,
Thy Cleopatra's waiting.
 [The shade of Antony disappears: another rises.
Arn.Who is this?
Who truly looketh like a demigod,
Blooming and bright, with golden hair, and stature,
If not more high than mortal, yet immortal
In all that nameless bearing of his limbs,250
Which he wears as the Sun his rays—a something
Which shines from him, and yet is but the flashing
Emanation of a thing more glorious still.
Was he e'er human only?[217][487]
Stran.Let the earth speak,
If there be atoms of him left, or even
Of the more solid gold that formed his urn.
Arn. Who was this glory of mankind?
Stran.The shame
Of Greece in peace, her thunderbolt in war—
Demetrius the Macedonian, and
Taker of cities.
Arn.Yet one shadow more.260
Stran. (addressing the shadow). Get thee to Lamia's lap!
 [The shade of Demetrius Poliorcetes vanishes: another rises.
I'll fit you still,
Fear not, my Hunchback: if the shadows of
That which existed please not your nice taste,
I'll animate the ideal marble, till
Your soul be reconciled to her new garment
Arn. Content! I will fix here.
Stran.I must commend
Your choice. The godlike son of the sea-goddess,

The unshorn boy of Peleus, with his locks
As beautiful and clear as the amber waves
Of rich Pactolus, rolled o'er sands of gold,270
Softened by intervening crystal, and
Rippled like flowing waters by the wind,[488]
All vowed to Sperchius[218] as they were — behold them!
And him — as he stood by Polixena,
With sanctioned and with softened love, before
The altar, gazing on his Trojan bride,
With some remorse within for Hector slain
And Priam weeping, mingled with deep passion
For the sweet downcast virgin, whose young hand
Trembled in his who slew her brother. So280
He stood i' the temple! Look upon him as
Greece looked her last upon her best, the instant
Ere Paris' arrow flew.
Arn.I gaze upon him
As if I were his soul, whose form shall soon
Envelope mine.
Stran.You have done well. The greatest
Deformity should only barter with
The extremest beauty — if the proverb's true
Of mortals, that Extremes meet.
Arn.Come! Be quick!
I am impatient.
Stran.As a youthful beauty
Before her glass. You both see what is not,290
But dream it is what must be.
Arn.Must I wait?
Stran. No; that were a pity. But a word or two:
His stature is twelve cubits; would you so far
Outstep these times, and be a Titan? Or
(To talk canonically) wax a son
Of Anak?
Arn.Why not?

Stran.Glorious ambition!
I love thee most in dwarfs! A mortal of
Philistine stature would have gladly pared
His own Goliath down to a slight David:
But thou, my manikin, wouldst soar a show300
Rather than hero. Thou shalt be indulged,[489]
If such be thy desire; and, yet, by being
A little less removed from present men
In figure, thou canst sway them more; for all
Would rise against thee now, as if to hunt
A new-found Mammoth; and their curséd engines,
Their culverins, and so forth, would find way
Through our friend's armour there, with greater ease
Than the Adulterer's arrow through his heel
Which Thetis had forgotten to baptize310
In Styx.
Arn.Then let it be as thou deem'st best.
Stran. Thou shalt be beauteous as the thing thou seest,
And strong as what it was, and — —
Arn.I ask not
For Valour, since Deformity is daring.[219]
It is its essence to o'ertake mankind
By heart and soul, and make itself the equal —
Aye, the superior of the rest. There is
A spur in its halt movements, to become
All that the others cannot, in such things
As still are free to both, to compensate320
For stepdame Nature's avarice at first.
They woo with fearless deeds the smiles of fortune,
And oft, like Timour the lame Tartar,[220] win them.
Stran. Well spoken! And thou doubtless wilt remain
Formed as thou art. I may dismiss the mould
Of shadow, which must turn to flesh, to incase
This daring soul, which could achieve no less
Without it.[490]

Arn.Had no power presented me
The possibility of change, I would
Have done the best which spirit may to make330
Its way with all Deformity's dull, deadly,
Discouraging weight upon me, like a mountain,
In feeling, on my heart as on my shoulders—
A hateful and unsightly molehill to
The eyes of happier men. I would have looked
On Beauty in that sex which is the type
Of all we know or dream of beautiful,
Beyond the world they brighten, with a sigh—
Not of love, but despair; nor sought to win,
Though to a heart all love, what could not love me340
In turn, because of this vile crookéd clog,
Which makes me lonely. Nay, I could have borne
It all, had not my mother spurned me from her.
The she-bear licks her cubs into a sort
Of shape;—my Dam beheld my shape was hopeless.
Had she exposed me, like the Spartan, ere
I knew the passionate part of life, I had
Been a clod of the valley,—happier nothing
Than what I am. But even thus—the lowest,
Ugliest, and meanest of mankind—what courage350
And perseverance could have done, perchance
Had made me something—as it has made heroes
Of the same mould as mine. You lately saw me
Master of my own life, and quick to quit it;
And he who is so is the master of
Whatever dreads to die.
Stran.Decide between
What you have been, or will be.
Arn.I have done so.
You have opened brighter prospects to my eyes,
And sweeter to my heart. As I am now,
I might be feared—admired—respected—loved360

Of all save those next to me, of whom I
Would be belovéd. As thou showest me
A choice of forms, I take the one I view.
Haste! haste!
Stran.And what shall I wear?
Arn.Surely, he[491]
Who can command all forms will choose the highest,
Something superior even to that which was
Pelides now before us. Perhaps his
Who slew him, that of Paris: or — still higher —
The Poet's God, clothed in such limbs as are
Themselves a poetry.
Stran.Less will content me;370
For I, too, love a change.
Arn.Your aspect is
Dusky, but not uncomely.[221]
Stran.If I chose,
I might be whiter; but I have a penchant
For black — it is so honest, and, besides,
Can neither blush with shame nor pale with fear;
But I have worn it long enough of late,
And now I'll take your figure.
Arn.Mine!
Stran.Yes. You
Shall change with Thetis' son, and I with Bertha,
Your mother's offspring. People have their tastes;
You have yours — I mine.
Arn.Despatch! despatch!
Stran.Even so.380
[The Stranger takes some earth and moulds it along the turf,
and then addresses the phantom of Achilles.
Beautiful shadow
Of Thetis's boy!
Who sleeps in the meadow
Whose grass grows o'er Troy:

From the red earth, like Adam,[222]
Thy likeness I shape,
As the Being who made him,
Whose actions I ape.
Thou Clay, be all glowing,
Till the Rose in his cheek390
Be as fair as, when blowing,
It wears its first streak![492]
Ye Violets, I scatter,
Now turn into eyes!
And thou, sunshiny Water,
Of blood take the guise!
Let these Hyacinth boughs
Be his long flowing hair,
And wave o'er his brows,
As thou wavest in air!400
Let his heart be this marble
I tear from the rock!
But his voice as the warble
Of birds on yon oak!
Let his flesh be the purest
Of mould, in which grew
The Lily-root surest,
And drank the best dew!
Let his limbs be the lightest
Which clay can compound,410
And his aspect the brightest
On earth to be found!
Elements, near me,
Be mingled and stirred,
Know me, and hear me,
And leap to my word!
Sunbeams, awaken
This earth's animation![dc]
'Tis done! He hath taken

His stand in creation!420

[ARNOLD falls senseless; his soul passes into the shape of Achilles, which rises from the ground; while the phantom has disappeared, part by part, as the figure was formed from the earth.

Arn. (in his new form). I love, and I shall be beloved! Oh, life!
At last I feel thee! Glorious Spirit!
Stran.Stop!
What shall become of your abandoned garment,
Yon hump, and lump, and clod of ugliness,
Which late you wore, or were?
Arn.Who cares? Let wolves[493]
And vultures take it, if they will.
Stran.And if
They do, and are not scared by it, you'll say
It must be peace-time, and no better fare
Abroad i' the fields.
Arn.Let us but leave it there;
No matter what becomes on't.
Stran.That's ungracious;430
If not ungrateful. Whatsoe'er it be,
It hath sustained your soul full many a day.
Arn. Aye, as the dunghill may conceal a gem
Which is now set in gold, as jewels should be.
Stran. But if I give another form, it must be
By fair exchange, not robbery. For they[223]
Who make men without women's aid have long
Had patents for the same, and do not love
Your Interlopers. The Devil may take men,[dd]
Not make them,—though he reap the benefit440
Of the original workmanship:—and therefore
Some one must be found to assume the shape
You have quitted.
Arn.Who would do so?
Stran.That I know not,

And therefore I must.
Arn.You!
Stran.I said it ere
You inhabited your present dome of beauty.
Arn. True. I forget all things in the new joy
Of this immortal change.
Stran.In a few moments
I will be as you were, and you shall see[494]
Yourself for ever by you, as your shadow.
Arn. I would be spared this.
Stran.But it cannot be.450
What! shrink already, being what you are,
From seeing what you were?
Arn.Do as thou wilt.
Stran. (to the late form of ARNOLD, extended on the earth).
Clay! not dead, but soul-less!
Though no man would choose thee,
An Immortal no less
Deigns not to refuse thee.
Clay thou art; and unto spirit
All clay is of equal merit.
Fire! without which nought can live;
Fire! but in which nought can live,460
Save the fabled salamander,
Or immortal souls, which wander,
Praying what doth not forgive,
Howling for a drop of water,
Burning in a quenchless lot:
Fire! the only element
Where nor fish, beast, bird, nor worm,
Save the Worm which dieth not,
Can preserve a moment's form,
But must with thyself be blent:470
Fire! man's safeguard and his slaughter:
Fire! Creation's first-born Daughter,

And Destruction's threatened Son,
When Heaven with the world hath done:
Fire! assist me to renew
Life in what lies in my view
Stiff and cold!
His resurrection rests with me and you!
One little, marshy spark of flame — [224]
And he again shall seem the same;480
But I his Spirit's place shall hold!
[495]
[An ignis-fatuus flits through the wood and rests on the brow
of the body. The Stranger disappears: the body rises.
Arn. (in his new form). Oh! horrible!
Stran. (in ARNOLD'S late shape). What! tremblest thou?
Arn.Not so —
I merely shudder. Where is fled the shape
Thou lately worest?
Stran.To the world of shadows.
But let us thread the present. Whither wilt thou?
Arn. Must thou be my companion?
Stran.Wherefore not?
Your betters keep worse company.
Arn.My betters!
Stran. Oh! you wax proud, I see, of your new form:
I'm glad of that. Ungrateful too! That's well;
You improve apace; — two changes in an instant,490
And you are old in the World's ways already.
But bear with me: indeed you'll find me useful
Upon your pilgrimage. But come, pronounce
Where shall we now be errant?
Arn.Where the World
Is thickest, that I may behold it in
Its workings.
Stran.That's to say, where there is War
And Woman in activity. Let's see!

Spain—Italy—the new Atlantic world[225]—
Afric with all its Moors. In very truth,
There is small choice: the whole race are just now500
Tugging as usual at each other's hearts.
Arn. I have heard great things of Rome.
Stran.A goodly choice—
And scarce a better to be found on earth,
Since Sodom was put out. The field is wide too;
For now the Frank, and Hun, and Spanish scion
Of the old Vandals, are at play along[496]
The sunny shores of the World's garden.
Arn.How
Shall we proceed?
Stran.Like gallants, on good coursers.
What, ho! my chargers! Never yet were better,
Since Phaeton was upset into the Po[226].510
Our pages too!
Enter two Pages, with four coal-black horses.
Arn.A noble sight!
Stran.And of
A nobler breed. Match me in Barbary,
Or your Kochlini race of Araby[de][227],
With these!
Arn.The mighty steam, which volumes high
From their proud nostrils, burns the very air;
And sparks of flame, like dancing fire-flies wheel
Around their manes, as common insects swarm
Round common steeds towards sunset.
Stran.Mount, my lord:
They and I are your servitors.
Arn.And these
Our dark-eyed pages—what may be their names?520
Stran. You shall baptize them.
Arn.What! in holy water?
Stran. Why not? The deeper sinner, better saint.

Arn. They are beautiful, and cannot, sure, be demons.
Stran. True; the devil's always ugly: and your beauty
Is never diabolical.
Arn.I'll call him
Who bears the golden horn, and wears such bright
And blooming aspect, Huon;[228] for he looks[497]
Like to the lovely boy lost in the forest,
And never found till now. And for the other
And darker, and more thoughtful, who smiles not,530
But looks as serious though serene as night,
He shall be Memnon[229], from the Ethiop king
Whose statue turns a harper once a day.
And you?
Stran.I have ten thousand names, and twice
As many attributes; but as I wear
A human shape, will take a human name.
Arn. More human than the shape (though it was mine once)
I trust.
Stran.  Then call me Cæsar.
Arn.Why, that name
Belongs to Empire, and has been but borne
By the World's lords.
Stran.And therefore fittest for540
The Devil in disguise—since so you deem me,
Unless you call me Pope instead.
Arn.Well, then,
Cæsar thou shalt be. For myself, my name
Shall be plain Arnold still.
Cæs.We'll add a title[df]—
"Count Arnold:" it hath no ungracious sound,
And will look well upon a billet-doux.
Arn. Or in an order for a battle-field.
Cæs. (sings).
To horse! to horse! my coal-black steed
Paws the ground and snuffs the air!

There's not a foal of Arab's breed550
More knows whom he must bear;[498]
On the hill he will not tire,
Swifter as it waxes higher;
In the marsh he will not slacken,
On the plain be overtaken;
In the wave he will not sink,
Nor pause at the brook's side to drink;
In the race he will not pant,
In the combat he'll not faint;
On the stones he will not stumble,560
Time nor toil shall make him humble;
In the stall he will not stiffen,
But be wingèd as a Griffin,
Only flying with his feet:
And will not such a voyage be sweet?
Shall our bonny black horses skim over the ground!
From the Alps to the Caucasus, ride we, or fly!
For we'll leave them behind in the glance of an eye.
 [They mount their horses, and disappear.

# SCENE II —A Camp before the walls of Rome.

ARNOLD and CÆSAR.
Cæs. You are well entered now.
Arn.Aye; but my path
Has been o'er carcasses: mine eyes are full[dg]
Of blood.
Cæs.Then wipe them, and see clearly. Why!
Thou art a conqueror; the chosen knight
And free companion of the gallant Bourbon,
Late constable of France[230]; and now to be[499]
Lord of the city which hath been Earth's Lord
Under its emperors, and—changing sex,
Not sceptre, an Hermaphrodite of Empire—
Lady of the old world[231].
Arn.How old? What! are there10
New worlds?
Cæs.To you. You'll find there are such shortly,
By its rich harvests, new disease, and gold;
From one half of the world named a whole new one,
Because you know no better than the dull
And dubious notice of your eyes and ears.
Arn. I'll trust them.
Cæs.Do! They will deceive you sweetly,
And that is better than the bitter truth.
Arn. Dog!
Cæs.Man!
Arn.Devil![500]
Cæs.Your obedient humble servant.
Arn. Say master rather. Thou hast lured me on,
Through scenes of blood and lust, till I am here.20

Cæs. And where wouldst thou be?
Arn.Oh, at peace—in peace!
Cæs. And where is that which is so? From the star
To the winding worm, all life is motion; and
In life commotion is the extremest point
Of life. The planet wheels till it becomes
A comet, and destroying as it sweeps
The stars, goes out. The poor worm winds its way,
Living upon the death of other things,
But still, like them, must live and die, the subject
Of something which has made it live and die.30
You must obey what all obey, the rule
Of fixed Necessity: against her edict
Rebellion prospers not.
Arn.And when it prospers— —
Cæs. 'Tis no rebellion.
Arn.Will it prosper now?
Cæs. The Bourbon hath given orders for the assault,
And by the dawn there will be work.
Arn.Alas!
And shall the city yield? I see the giant
Abode of the true God, and his true saint,
Saint Peter, rear its dome and cross into
That sky whence Christ ascended from the cross,40
Which his blood made a badge of glory and
Of joy (as once of torture unto him),—
God and God's Son, man's sole and only refuge!
Cæs. 'Tis there, and shall be.
Arn.What?
Cæs.The Crucifix
Above, and many altar shrines below.
Also some culverins upon the walls,
And harquebusses, and what not; besides
The men who are to kindle them to death
Of other men.

Arn.And those scarce mortal arches,[232][501]
Pile above pile of everlasting wall,50
The theatre where Emperors and their subjects
(Those subjects Romans) stood at gaze upon
The battles of the monarchs of the wild
And wood—the lion and his tusky rebels
Of the then untamed desert, brought to joust
In the arena—as right well they might,
When they had left no human foe unconquered—
Made even the forest pay its tribute of
Life to their amphitheatre, as well
As Dacia men to die the eternal death60
For a sole instant's pastime, and "Pass on
To a new gladiator!"—Must it fall?
Cæs. The city, or the amphitheatre?
The church, or one, or all? for you confound
Both them and me.
Arn.To-morrow sounds the assault
With the first cock-crow.
Cæs.Which, if it end with
The evening's first nightingale, will be
Something new in the annals of great sieges;
For men must have their prey after long toil.
Arn. The sun goes down as calmly, and perhaps70
More beautifully, than he did on Rome
On the day Remus leapt her wall.
Cæs.I saw him.
Arn. You!
Cæs.Yes, Sir! You forget I am or was
Spirit, till I took up with your cast shape,
And a worse name. I'm Cæsar and a hunch-back
Now. Well! the first of Cæsars was a bald-head,
And loved his laurels better as a wig
(So history says) than as a glory.[233] Thus
The world runs on, but we'll be merry still.

I saw your Romulus (simple as I am)80
Slay his own twin, quick-born of the same womb,
Because he leapt a ditch ('twas then no wall,[502]
Whate'er it now be); and Rome's earliest cement
Was brother's blood; and if its native blood
Be spilt till the choked Tiber be as red
As e'er 'twas yellow, it will never wear
The deep hue of the Ocean and the Earth,
Which the great robber sons of fratricide
Have made their never-ceasing scene of slaughter,
For ages.
Arn.But what have these done, their far90
Remote descendants, who have lived in peace,
The peace of Heaven, and in her sunshine of
Piety?
Cæs. And what had they done, whom the old
Romans o'erswept? — Hark!
Arn.They are soldiers singing
A reckless roundelay, upon the eve
Of many deaths, it may be of their own.
Cæs. And why should they not sing as well as swans?
They are black ones, to be sure.
Arn.So, you are learned,
I see, too?
Cæs.In my grammar, certes. I
Was educated for a monk of all times,100
And once I was well versed in the forgotten
Etruscan letters, and — were I so minded —
Could make their hieroglyphics plainer than
Your alphabet.
Arn.And wherefore do you not?
Cæs. It answers better to resolve the alphabet
Back into hieroglyphics. Like your statesman,
And prophet, pontiff, doctor, alchymist,
Philosopher, and what not, they have built

More Babels, without new dispersion, than
The stammering young ones of the flood's dull ooze,110
Who failed and fled each other. Why? why, marry,
Because no man could understand his neighbour.
They are wiser now, and will not separate
For nonsense. Nay, it is their brotherhood,
Their Shibboleth—their Koran—Talmud—their
Cabala—their best brick-work, wherewithal
They build more——[503]
Arn. (interrupting him). Oh, thou everlasting sneerer!
Be silent! How the soldier's rough strain seems
Softened by distance to a hymn-like cadence!
Listen!
Cæs.Yes. I have heard the angels sing.120
Arn. And demons howl.
Cæs.And man, too. Let us listen:
I love all music.
Song of the Soldiers within.
The black bands came over
The Alps and their snow;
With Bourbon, the rover,
They passed the broad Po.
We have beaten all foemen,
We have captured a King[234],
We have turned back on no men,
And so let us sing!130
Here's the Bourbon for ever!
Though penniless all,
We'll have one more endeavour
At yonder old wall.
With the Bourbon we'll gather
At day-dawn before
The gates, and together
Or break or climb o'er
The wall: on the ladder,

As mounts each firm foot[dh],140
Our shout shall grow gladder,
And Death only be mute[235].
With the Bourbon we'll mount o'er
The walls of old Rome,
And who then shall count o'er[di]
The spoils of each dome?[504]
Up! up with the Lily!
And down with the Keys!
In old Rome, the seven-hilly,
We'll revel at ease.150
Her streets shall be gory,
Her Tiber all red,
And her temples so hoary
Shall clang with our tread.
Oh, the Bourbon! the Bourbon[236]!
The Bourbon for aye!
Of our song bear the burden!
And fire, fire away!
With Spain for the vanguard,
Our varied host comes;160
And next to the Spaniard
Beat Germany's drums;
And Italy's lances
Are couched at their mother;
But our leader from France is,
Who warred with his brother.
Oh, the Bourbon! the Bourbon!
Sans country or home,
We'll follow the Bourbon,
To plunder old Rome.170
Cæs.An indifferent song
For those within the walls, methinks, to hear.
Arn. Yes, if they keep to their chorus. But here comes
The general with his chiefs and men of trust[dj].

A goodly rebel.
Enter the Constable BOURBON "cum suis," etc., etc.
Phil.How now, noble Prince,
You are not cheerful?
Bourb.Why should I be so?
Phil. Upon the eve of conquest, such as ours,
Most men would be so.[505]
Bourb.If I were secure!
Phil. Doubt not our soldiers. Were the walls of adamant,
They'd crack them. Hunger is a sharp artillery.180
Bourb. That they will falter is my least of fears.
That they will be repulsed, with Bourbon for
Their chief, and all their kindled appetites
To marshal them on — were those hoary walls
Mountains, and those who guard them like the gods
Of the old fables, I would trust my Titans; —
But now — —
Phil.They are but men who war with mortals.
Bourb. True: but those walls have girded in great ages,
And sent forth mighty spirits. The past earth
And present phantom of imperious Rome[dk]190
Is peopled with those warriors; and methinks
They flit along the eternal City's rampart,
And stretch their glorious, gory, shadowy hands,
And beckon me away!
Phil.So let them! Wilt thou
Turn back from shadowy menaces of shadows?
Bourb. They do not menace me. I could have faced,
Methinks, a Sylla's menace; but they clasp,
And raise, and wring their dim and deathlike hands,
And with their thin aspen faces and fixed eyes
Fascinate mine. Look there!
Phil.I look upon200
A lofty battlement.
Bourb.And there!

Phil.Not even
A guard in sight; they wisely keep below,
Sheltered by the grey parapet from some
Stray bullet of our lansquenets, who might
Practise in the cool twilight.
Bourb.You are blind.
Phil. If seeing nothing more than may be seen
Be so.
Bourb. A thousand years have manned the walls[506]
With all their heroes,—the last Cato[237] stands
And tears his bowels, rather than survive
The liberty of that I would enslave.210
And the first Cassar with his triumphs flits
From battlement to battlement.
Phil.Then conquer
The walls for which he conquered and be greater!
Bourb. True: so I will, or perish.
Phil.You can not.
In such an enterprise to die is rather
The dawn of an eternal day, than death.
 [Count ARNOLD and CÆSAR advance.
Cæs. And the mere men—do they, too, sweat beneath
The noon of this same ever-scorching glory?
Bourb.Ah!
Welcome the bitter Hunchback! and his master,
The beauty of our host, and brave as beauteous,220
And generous as lovely. We shall find
Work for you both ere morning.
Cæs.You will find,
So please your Highness, no less for yourself.
Bourb. And if I do, there will not be a labourer
More forward, Hunchback!
Cæs.You may well say so,
For you have seen that back—as general,
Placed in the rear in action—but your foes

Have never seen it.

Bourb.That's a fair retort,
For I provoked it: — but the Bourbon's breast
Has been, and ever shall be, far advanced230
In danger's face as yours, were you the devil.

Cæs. And if I were, I might have saved myself
The toil of coming here.

Phil.Why so?

Cæs.One half[507]
Of your brave bands of their own bold accord
Will go to him, the other half be sent,
More swiftly, not less surely.

Bourb.Arnold, your
Slight crooked friend's as snake-like in his words
As his deeds.

Cæs.Your Highness much mistakes me.
The first snake was a flatterer — I am none;
And for my deeds, I only sting when stung.240

Bourb. You are brave, and that's enough for me; and quick
In speech as sharp in action — and that's more.
I am not alone the soldier, but the soldiers'
Comrade.

Cæs.They are but bad company, your Highness;
And worse even for their friends than foes, as being
More permanent acquaintance.

Phil.How now, fellow!
Thou waxest insolent, beyond the privilege
Of a buffoon.

Cæs.You mean I speak the truth.
I'll lie — it is as easy: then you'll praise me
For calling you a hero.

Bourb.Philibert!250
Let him alone; he's brave, and ever has
Been first, with that swart face and mountain shoulder,
In field or storm, and patient in starvation;

And for his tongue, the camp is full of licence,
And the sharp stinging of a lively rogue
Is, to my mind, far preferable to
The gross, dull, heavy, gloomy execration
Of a mere famished sullen grumbling slave,[dl]
Whom nothing can convince save a full meal,
And wine, and sleep, and a few Maravedis,260
With which he deems him rich.
Cæs.It would be well
If the earth's princes asked no more.
Bourb.Be silent!
Cæs. Aye, but not idle. Work yourself with words![dm][508]
You have few to speak.
Phil.What means the audacious prater?
Cæs. To prate, like other prophets.
Bourb.Philibert!
Why will you vex him? Have we not enough
To think on? Arnold! I will lead the attack
To-morrow.
Arn.I have heard as much, my Lord.
Bourb. And you will follow?
Arn.Since I must not lead.
Bourb. 'Tis necessary for the further daring
Of our too needy army, that their chief
Plant the first foot upon the foremost ladder's
First step.
Cæs.Upon its topmost, let us hope:
So shall he have his full deserts.
Bourb.The world's
Great capital perchance is ours to-morrow.[dn]
Through every change the seven-hilled city hath
Retained her sway o'er nations, and the Cæsars
But yielded to the Alarics, the Alarics
Unto the pontiffs. Roman, Goth, or priest.
Still the world's masters! Civilised, barbarian,

Or saintly, still the walls of Romulus
Have been the circus of an Empire. Well!
'Twas their turn—now 'tis ours; and let us hope
That we will fight as well, and rule much better.
Cæs. No doubt, the camp's the school of civic rights.
What would you make of Rome?
Bourb.That which it was.
Cæs. In Alaric's time?
Bourb.No, slave! in the first Cæsar's,
Whose name you bear like other curs——
Cæs.And kings!
'Tis a great name for blood-hounds.
Bourb.There's a demon
In that fierce rattlesnake thy tongue. Wilt never
Be serious?
Cæs.On the eve of battle, no;—
That were not soldier-like. 'Tis for the general[509]
To be more pensive: we adventurers
Must be more cheerful. Wherefore should we think?
Our tutelar Deity, in a leader's shape,
Takes care of us. Keep thought aloof from hosts!
If the knaves take to thinking, you will have
To crack those walls alone.
Bourb.You may sneer, since
'Tis lucky for you that you fight no worse for 't.
Cæs. I thank you for the freedom; 'tis the only300
Pay I have taken in your Highness' service.
Bourb. Well, sir, to-morrow you shall pay yourself.
Look on those towers; they hold my treasury:
But, Philibert, we'll in to council. Arnold,
We would request your presence.
Arn.Prince! my service
Is yours, as in the field.
Bourb.In both we prize it,
And yours will be a post of trust at daybreak.

Cæs. And mine?
Bourb.To follow glory with the Bourbon.
Good night!
Arn. (to CÆSAR). Prepare our armour for the assault,
And wait within my tent.
 [Exeunt BOURBON, ARNOLD, PHILIBERT, etc.
Cæs. (solus).Within thy tent!310
Think'st thou that I pass from thee with my presence?
Or that this crooked coffer, which contained
Thy principle of life, is aught to me
Except a mask? And these are men, forsooth!
Heroes and chiefs, the flower of Adam's bastards!
This is the consequence of giving matter
The power of thought. It is a stubborn substance,
And thinks chaotically, as it acts,
Ever relapsing into its first elements.
Well! I must play with these poor puppets: 'tis320
The Spirit's pastime in his idler hours.
When I grow weary of it, I have business
Amongst the stars, which these poor creatures deem
Were made for them to look at. 'Twere a jest now
To bring one down amongst them, and set fire
Unto their anthill: how the pismires then[510]
Would scamper o'er the scalding soil, and, ceasing
From tearing down each other's nests, pipe forth
One universal orison! ha! ha![Exit CAESAR.

# PART II.

## SCENE I —Before the walls of Rome.—The Assault: the Army in motion, with ladders to scale the walls; BOURBON with a white scarf over his armour, foremost.

Chorus of Spirits in the air.
I.
'Tis the morn, but dim and dark.[do]
Whither flies the silent lark?
Whither shrinks the clouded sun?
Is the day indeed begun?
Nature's eye is melancholy
O'er the city high and holy:
But without there is a din
Should arouse the saints within,
And revive the heroic ashes
Round which yellow Tiber dashes.10
Oh, ye seven hills! awaken,
Ere your very base be shaken!
II.
Hearken to the steady stamp!
Mars is in their every tramp![511]
Not a step is out of tune,
As the tides obey the moon!
On they march, though to self-slaughter,
Regular as rolling water,
Whose high-waves o'ersweep the border
Of huge moles, but keep their order,20
Breaking only rank by rank.
Hearken to the armour's clank!

Look down o'er each frowning warrior,
How he glares upon the barrier:
Look on each step of each ladder,
As the stripes that streak an adder.
III.
Look upon the bristling wall,
Manned without an interval!
Round and round, and tier on tier,
Cannon's black mouth, shining spear,30
Lit match, bell-mouthed Musquetoon,
Gaping to be murderous soon;
All the warlike gear of old,
Mixed with what we now behold,
In this strife 'twixt old and new,
Gather like a locusts' crew.
Shade of Remus! 'tis a time
Awful as thy brother's crime!
Christians war against Christ's shrine:—
Must its lot be like to thine?40
IV.
Near—and near—and nearer still,
As the Earthquake saps the hill,
First with trembling, hollow motion,
Like a scarce awakened ocean,
Then with stronger shock and louder,
Till the rocks are crushed to powder,—
Onward sweeps the rolling host!
Heroes of the immortal boast!
Mighty Chiefs! eternal shadows!
First flowers of the bloody meadows50[512]
Which encompass Rome, the mother
Of a people without brother!
Will you sleep when nations' quarrels
Plough the root up of your laurels?
Ye who weep o'er Carthage burning,

Weep not—strike! for Rome is mourning![239]
V.
Onward sweep the varied nations!
Famine long hath dealt their rations.
To the wall, with hate and hunger,
Numerous as wolves, and stronger,60
On they sweep. Oh, glorious City!
Must thou be a theme for pity?
Fight, like your first sire, each Roman!
Alaric was a gentle foeman,
Matched with Bourbon's black banditti!
Rouse thee, thou eternal City;
Rouse thee! Rather give the torch
With thine own hand to thy porch,[dp]
Than behold such hosts pollute
Your worst dwelling with their foot.70
VI.
Ah! behold yon bleeding spectre!
Ilion's children find no Hector;
Priam's offspring loved their brother;
Rome's great sire forgot his mother,
When he slew his gallant twin,
With inexpiable sin.
See the giant shadow stride
O'er the ramparts high and wide!
When the first o'erleapt thy wall,
Its foundation mourned thy fall.80
Now, though towering like a Babel,
Who to stop his steps are able?[513]
Stalking o'er thy highest dome,
Remus claims his vengeance, Rome!
VII.
Now they reach thee in their anger:
Fire and smoke and hellish clangour
Are around thee, thou world's wonder!

Death is in thy walls and under.
Now the meeting steel first clashes,
Downward then the ladder crashes,90
With its iron load all gleaming,
Lying at its foot blaspheming!
Up again! for every warrior
Slain, another climbs the barrier.
Thicker grows the strife: thy ditches
Europe's mingling gore enriches.
Rome! although thy wall may perish,
Such manure thy fields will cherish,
Making gay the harvest-home;
But thy hearths, alas! oh, Rome!—100
Yet be Rome amidst thine anguish,
Fight as thou wast wont to vanquish!
VIII.
Yet once more, ye old Penates!
Let not your quenched hearts be Atés!
Yet again, ye shadowy Heroes,
Yield not to these stranger Neros!
Though the son who slew his mother
Shed Rome's blood, he was your brother:
'Twas the Roman curbed the Roman;—
Brennus was a baffled foeman.110
Yet again, ye saints and martyrs,
Rise! for yours are holier charters!
Mighty Gods of temples falling,
Yet in ruin still appalling!
Mightier Founders of those altars,
True and Christian,—strike the assaulters!
Tiber! Tiber! let thy torrent
Show even Nature's self abhorrent.[514]
Let each breathing heart dilated
Turn, as doth the lion baited!120
Rome be crashed to one wide tomb,

But be still the Roman's Rome![240]
[BOURBON, ARNOLD, CÆSAR, and others, arrive at the foot
of the wall. ARNOLD is about to plant his ladder.
Bourb. Hold, Arnold! I am first.
Arn.Not so, my Lord.
Bourb. Hold, sir, I charge you! Follow! I am proud
Of such a follower, but will brook no leader.
  [BOURBON plants his ladder, and begins to mount.
Now, boys! On! on!
  [A shot strikes him, and BOURBON falls.
Cæs.And off!
Arn.Eternal powers!
The host will be appalled,—but vengeance! vengeance!
Bourb. 'Tis nothing—lend me your hand.
[BOURBON takes ARNOLD by the hand, and rises; but as he
puts his foot on the step, falls again.
Arnold! I am sped.
Conceal my fall[241]—all will go well—conceal it!
Fling my cloak o'er what will be dust anon;130
Let not the soldiers see it.
Arn.You must be
Removed; the aid of — —
Bourb.No, my gallant boy!
Death is upon me. But what is one life?
The Bourbon's spirit shall command them still.
Keep them yet ignorant that I am but clay,
Till they are conquerors—then do as you may.[515]
Cæs. Would not your Highness choose to kiss the cross?
We have no priest here, but the hilt of sword
May serve instead:—it did the same for Bayard[242].
Bourb. Thou bitter slave! to name him at this time!140
But I deserve it.
Arn. (to CÆSAR). Villain, hold your peace!
Cæs. What, when a Christian dies? Shall I not offer
A Christian "Vade in pace?"[243]

Arn.Silence! Oh!
Those eyes are glazing which o'erlooked the world,
And saw no equal.
Bourb.Arnold, shouldst thou see
France — — But hark! hark! the assault grows warmer — Oh!
For but an hour, a minute more of life,
To die within the wall! Hence, Arnold, hence!
You lose time — they will conquer Rome without thee.
Arn. And without thee.
Bourb.Not so; I'll lead them still150
In spirit. Cover up my dust, and breathe not
That I have ceased to breathe. Away! and be
Victorious.
Arn.But I must not leave thee thus.
Bourb. You must — farewell — Up! up! the world is winning.
 [BOURBON dies.
Cæs. (to ARNOLD). Come, Count, to business.
Arn.True. I'll weep hereafter.
[ARNOLD covers BOURBON'S body with a mantle, mounts
the ladder, crying
The Bourbon! Bourbon! On, boys! Rome is ours!
Cæs. Good night, Lord Constable! thou wert a Man.
[CÆSAR follows ARNOLD; they reach the battlement;
ARNOLD and CÆSAR are struck down.[516]
Cæs. A precious somerset! Is your countship injured?
Arn. No.[Remounts the ladder.
Cæs.A rare blood-hound, when his own is heated!
And 'tis no boy's play. Now he strikes them down!160
His hand is on the battlement — he grasps it
As though it were an altar; now his foot
Is on it, and — — What have we here? — a Roman?
The first bird of the covey! he has fallen[A man falls.
On the outside of the nest. Why, how now, fellow?
Wounded Man. A drop of water!
Cæs.Blood's the only liquid

Nearer than Tiber.
Wounded Man.I have died for Rome.[Dies.
Cæs. And so did Bourbon, in another sense.
Oh, these immortal men! and their great motives!
But I must after my young charge. He is170
By this time i' the Forum. Charge! charge!
 [CÆSAR mounts the ladder; the scene closes.

# SCENE II —The City.—Combats between the Besiegers and Besieged in the streets. Inhabitants flying in confusion.

Enter CÆSAR.
Cæs. I cannot find my hero; he is mixed
With the heroic crowd that now pursue
The fugitives, or battle with the desperate.
What have we here? A Cardinal or two
That do not seem in love with martyrdom.
How the old red-shanks scamper! Could they doff
Their hose as they have doffed their hats, 'twould be
A blessing, as a mark[244] the less for plunder.
But let them fly; the crimson kennels now
Will not much stain their stockings, since the mire10
Is of the self-same purple hue.
[517]
Enter a Party fighting — ARNOLD at the head of the Besiegers.
He comes,
Hand in hand with the mild twins — Gore and Glory.[dq]
Holla! hold, Count!
Arn. Away! they must not rally.
Cæs. I tell thee, be not rash; a golden bridge
Is for a flying enemy. I gave thee
A form of beauty, and an
Exemption from some maladies of body,
But not of mind, which is not mine to give.
But though I gave the form of Thetis' son,
I dipped thee not in Styx; and 'gainst a foe20
I would not warrant thy chivalric heart
More than Pelides' heel; why, then, be cautious,

And know thyself a mortal still.

Arn.And who
With aught of soul would combat if he were
Invulnerable? That were pretty sport.
Think'st thou I beat for hares when lions roar?

  [ARNOLD rushes into the combat.

Cæs. A precious sample of humanity!
Well, his blood's up; and, if a little's shed,
'Twill serve to curb his fever.

[ARNOLD engages with a Roman, who retires towards a portico.

Arn.Yield thee, slave!
I promise quarter.

Rom.That's soon said.

Arn.And done— —30
My word is known.

Rom.So shall be my deeds.

  [They re-engage. CÆSAR comes forward.

Cæs. Why, Arnold! hold thine own: thou hast in hand
A famous artisan, a cunning sculptor;
Also a dealer in the sword and dagger.
Not so, my musqueteer; 'twas he who slew
The Bourbon from the wall.[245][518]

Arn.Aye, did he so?
Then he hath carved his monument.

Rom.I yet
May live to carve your better's.

Cæs. Well said, my man of marble! Benvenuto,
Thou hast some practice in both ways; and he40
Who slays Cellini will have worked as hard
As e'er thou didst upon Carrara's blocks.

[ARNOLD disarms and wounds CELLINI, hit slightly: the latter draws a pistol, and fires; then retires, and disappears through the portico.

Cæs. How farest thou? Thou hast a taste, methinks,

Of red Bellona's banquet.
Arn. (staggers).'Tis a scratch.
Lend me thy scarf. He shall not 'scape me thus.
Cæs. Where is it?
Arn.In the shoulder, not the sword arm—
And that's enough. I am thirsty: would I had
A helm of water!
Cæs.That's a liquid now
In requisition, but by no means easiest
To come at.
Arn.And my thirst increases;—but50
I'll find a way to quench it.
Cæs.Or be quenched
Thyself.
Arn.The chance is even; we will throw
The dice thereon. But I lose time in prating;
Prithee be quick.[CÆSAR binds on the scarf.
And what dost thou so idly?
Why dost not strike?[519]
Cæs.Your old philosophers
Beheld mankind, as mere spectators of
The Olympic games. When I behold a prize
Worth wrestling for, I may be found a Milo.[246]
Arn. Aye, 'gainst an oak.
Cæs.A forest, when it suits me:
I combat with a mass, or not at all.60
Meantime, pursue thy sport as I do mine;
Which is just now to gaze, since all these labourers
Will reap my harvest gratis.
Arn.Thou art still
A fiend!
Cæs.And thou—a man.
Arn. Why, such I fain would show me.[dr]
Cæs.True—as men are.
Arn. And what is that?

Cæs.Thou feelest and thou see'st.
[Exit ARNOLD, joining in the combat which still continues between detached parties. The scene closes.

## SCENE III  —St. Peter's—The interior of the Church—The Pope at the Altar—Priests, etc., crowding in confusion, and Citizens flying for refuge, pursued by Soldiery.

Enter CÆSAR.
A Spanish Soldier. Down with them, comrades, seize upon those lamps!
Cleave yon bald-pated shaveling to the chine!
His rosary's of gold!
Lutheran Soldier.Revenge! revenge!
Plunder hereafter, but for vengeance now—
Yonder stands Anti-Christ!
Cæs. (interposing).How now, schismatic?
What wouldst thou?[520]
Luth. Sold.In the holy name of Christ,
Destroy proud Anti-Christ.[247] I am a Christian.
Cæs. Yea, a disciple that would make the founder
Of your belief renounce it, could he see
Such proselytes. Best stint thyself to plunder.10
Luth. Sold. I say he is the Devil.
Cæs.Hush! keep that secret,[ds]
Lest he should recognise you for his own.
Luth. Sold. Why would you save him? I repeat he is
The Devil, or the Devil's vicar upon earth.
Cæs. And that's the reason: would you make a quarrel
With your best friends? You had far best be quiet;
His hour is not yet come.
Luth. Sold.That shall be seen!

[The Lutheran Soldier rushes forward: a shot strikes him from one of the Pope's Guards, and he falls at the foot of the Altar.

Cæs. (to the Lutheran). I told you so.

Luth. Sold.And will you not avenge me?[521]

Cæs. Not I! You know that "Vengeance is the Lord's:"
You see he loves no interlopers.

Luth. Sold. (dying).Oh!20
Had I but slain him, I had gone on high,
Crowned with eternal glory! Heaven, forgive
My feebleness of arm that reached him not,
And take thy servant to thy mercy. 'Tis
A glorious triumph still; proud Babylon's
No more; the Harlot of the Seven Hills
Hath changed her scarlet raiment for sackcloth
And ashes![The Lutheran dies.

Cæs.Yes, thine own amidst the rest.
Well done, old Babel!

[The Guards defend themselves desperately, while the Pontiff escapes, by a private passage, to the Vatican and the Castle of St. Angelo.[248]

Cæs.Ha! right nobly battled!
Now, priest! now, soldier! the two great professions,30
Together by the ears and hearts! I have not
Seen a more comic pantomime since Titus
Took Jewry. But the Romans had the best then;
Now they must take their turn.

Soldiers.He hath escaped!
Follow!

Another Sold. They have barred the narrow passage up,
And it is clogged with dead even to the door.

Cæs. I am glad he hath escaped: he may thank me for't
In part. I would not have his bulls abolished —
'Twere worth one half our empire: his indulgences
Demand some in return; no, no, he must not40
Fall; — and besides, his now escape may furnish

A future miracle, in future proof[522]
Of his infallibility.[To the Spanish Soldiery.
Well, cut-throats!
What do you pause for? If you make not haste,
There will not be a link of pious gold left.
And you, too, Catholics! Would ye return
From such a pilgrimage without a relic?
The very Lutherans have more true devotion:
See how they strip the shrines!
Soldiers.By holy Peter!
He speaks the truth; the heretics will bear50
The best away.
Cæs.And that were shame! Go to!
Assist in their conversion.
[The Soldiers disperse; many quit the Church, others enter.
Cæs.They are gone,
And others come: so flows the wave on wave
Of what these creatures call Eternity,
Deeming themselves the breakers of the Ocean,
While they are but its bubbles, ignorant
That foam is their foundation. So, another!
Enter OLIMPIA, flying from the pursuit—She springs upon
the Altar.
Sold. She's mine!
Another Sold. (opposing the former).
You lie, I tracked her first: and were she
The Pope's niece, I'll not yield her.[They fight.
3d Sold. (advancing towards OLIMPIA). You may settle
Your claims; I'll make mine good.
Olimp.Infernal slave!60
You touch me not alive.
3d Sold.Alive or dead!
Olimp. (embracing a massive crucifix).    Respect your God!
3d Sold. Yes, when he shines in gold.
Girl, you but grasp your dowry.

[As he advances, OLIMPIA, with a strong and sudden effort,
casts down the crucifix; it strikes the Soldier, who falls.[523]
3d Sold.Oh, great God!
Olimp. Ah! now you recognise him.
3d Sold.My brain's crushed!
Comrades, help, ho! All's darkness![He dies.
Other Soldiers (coming up).
Slay her, although she had a thousand lives:
She hath killed our comrade.
Olimp.Welcome such a death!
You have no life to give, which the worst slave
Would take. Great God! through thy redeeming Son,
And thy Son's Mother, now receive me as70
I would approach thee, worthy her, and him, and thee!
Enter ARNOLD.
Arn. What do I see? Accurséd jackals! Forbear!
Cæs. (aside and laughing). Ha! ha! here's equity! The dogs
Have as much right as he. But to the issue!
Soldiers. Count, she hath slain our comrade.
Arn.With what weapon?
Sold. The cross, beneath which he is crushed; behold him
Lie there, more like a worm than man; she cast it
Upon his head.
Arn.Even so: there is a woman
Worthy a brave man's liking. Were ye such,
Ye would have honoured her. But get ye hence,80
And thank your meanness, other God you have none,
For your existence. Had you touched a hair
Of those dishevelled locks, I would have thinned
Your ranks more than the enemy. Away!
Ye jackals! gnaw the bones the lion leaves,
But not even these till he permits.
A Sold. (murmuring).The lion
Might conquer for himself then.
Arn. (cuts him down).Mutineer!

Rebel in hell — you shall obey on earth!
[The Soldiers assault ARNOLD.
Arn. Come on! I'm glad on't! I will show you, slaves,[524]
How you should be commanded, and who led you90
First o'er the wall you were so shy to scale,
Until I waved my banners from its height,
As you are bold within it.
[ARNOLD mows down the foremost; the rest throw down
their arms.
Soldiers.Mercy! mercy!
Arn. Then learn to grant it. Have I taught you who
Led you o'er Rome's eternal battlements?
Soldiers. We saw it, and we know it; yet forgive
A moment's error in the heat of conquest —
The conquest which you led to.
Arn.Get you hence!
Hence to your quarters! you will find them fixed
In the Colonna palace.
Olimp. (aside).In my father's100
House!
Arn. (to the Soldiers). Leave your arms; ye have no further
need
Of such: the city's rendered. And mark well
You keep your hands clean, or I'll find out a stream
As red as Tiber now runs, for your baptism.
Soldiers (deposing their arms and departing). We obey!
Arn. (to OLIMPIA). Lady, you are safe.
Olimp.I should be so,
Had I a knife even; but it matters not —
Death hath a thousand gates; and on the marble,
Even at the altar foot, whence I look down
Upon destruction, shall my head be dashed,
Ere thou ascend it. God forgive thee, man!110
Arn. I wish to merit his forgiveness, and
Thine own, although I have not injured thee.

Olimp. No! Thou hast only sacked my native land, —
No injury! —and made my father's house
A den of thieves! No injury! —this temple—
Slippery with Roman and with holy gore!
No injury! And now thou wouldst preserve me,
To be— —but that shall never be!
[She raises her eyes to Heaven, folds her robe round her, and
prepares to dash herself down on the side of the Altar
opposite to that where ARNOLD stands.[525]
Arn.Hold! hold!
I swear.
Olimp.Spare thine already forfeit soul
A perjury for which even Hell would loathe thee.120
I know thee.
Arn.No, thou know'st me not; I am not
Of these men, though— —
Olimp.I judge thee by thy mates;
It is for God to judge thee as thou art.
I see thee purple with the blood of Rome;
Take mine, 'tis all thou e'er shalt have of me,
And here, upon the marble of this temple,
Where the baptismal font baptized me God's,
I offer him a blood less holy
But not less pure (pure as it left me then,
A redeeméd infant) than the holy water130
The saints have sanctified!
[OLIMPIA waves her hand to ARNOLD with disdain, and
dashes herself on the pavement from the Altar.
Arn.Eternal God!
I feel thee now! Help! help! she's gone.
Cæs. (approaches).I am here.
Arn. Thou! but oh, save her!
Cæs. (assisting him to raise OLIMPIA). She hath done it well!
The leap was serious.
Arn.Oh! she is lifeless!

Cæs.If
She be so, I have nought to do with that:
The resurrection is beyond me.
Arn.Slave!
Cæs. Aye, slave or master, 'tis all one: methinks
Good words, however, are as well at times.
Arn. Words!—Canst thou aid her?
Cæs.I will try. A sprinkling
Of that same holy water may be useful.140
 [He brings some in his helmet from the font.
Arn. 'Tis mixed with blood.
Cæs.There is no cleaner now
In Rome.[526]
Arn. How pale! how beautiful! how lifeless!
Alive or dead, thou Essence of all Beauty,
I love but thee!
Cæs.Even so Achilles loved
Penthesilea;[249] with his form it seems
You have his heart, and yet it was no soft one.
Arn. She breathes! But no, 'twas nothing, or the last
Faint flutter Life disputes with Death.
Cæs.She breathes.
Arn. Thou say'st it? Then 'tis truth.
Cæs.You do me right—
The Devil speaks truth much oftener than he's deemed:150
He hath an ignorant audience.
Arn. (without attending to him). Yes! her heart beats.
Alas! that the first beat of the only heart
I ever wished to beat with mine should vibrate
To an assassin's pulse.
Cæs.A sage reflection,
But somewhat late i' the day. Where shall we bear her?
I say she lives.
Arn.And will she live?
Cas.As much

As dust can.
Arn.Then she is dead!
Cæs.Bah! bah! You are so,
And do not know it. She will come to life—
Such as you think so, such as you now are;
But we must work by human means.
Arn.We will160
Convey her unto the Colonna palace,
Where I have pitched my banner.
Cæs.Come then! raise her up!
Arn. Softly!
Cæs.As softly as they bear the dead,
Perhaps because they cannot feel the jolting.
Arn. But doth she live indeed?
Cæs.Nay, never fear!
But, if you rue it after, blame not me.[527]
Arn. Let her but live!
Cæs.The Spirit of her life
Is yet within her breast, and may revive.
Count! count! I am your servant in all things,
And this is a new office:—'tis not oft170
I am employed in such; but you perceive
How staunch a friend is what you call a fiend.
On earth you have often only fiends for friends;
Now I desert not mine. Soft! bear her hence,
The beautiful half-clay, and nearly spirit!
I am almost enamoured of her, as
Of old the Angels of her earliest sex.[250]
Arn. Thou!
Cæs.I! But fear not. I'll not be your rival.
Arn. Rival!
Cæs.I could be one right formidable;
But since I slew the seven husbands of180
Tobias' future bride (and after all
Was smoked out by some incense),[251] I have laid

Aside intrigue: 'tis rarely worth the trouble
Of gaining, or—what is more difficult—
Getting rid of your prize again; for there's
The rub! at least to mortals.
Arn.Prithee, peace!
Softly! methinks her lips move, her eyes open!
Cæs. Like stars, no doubt; for that's a metaphor
For Lucifer and Venus.
Arn.To the palace
Colonna, as I told you!
Cæs.Oh! I know190
My way through Rome.
Arn.Now onward, onward! Gently!
 [Exeunt, bearing OLIMPIA. The scene closes.
[528]

# PART III.

# SCENE I —A Castle in the Apennines, surrounded by a wild but smiling Country. Chorus of Peasants singing before the Gates.

Chorus.
I.
The wars are over,
The spring is come;
The bride and her lover
Have sought their home:
They are happy, we rejoice;
Let their hearts have an echo in every voice!
II.
The spring is come; the violet's gone,
The first-born child of the early sun:[dt]
With us she is but a winter's flower,
The snow on the hills cannot blast her bower,10
And she lifts up her dewy eye of blue
To the youngest sky of the self-same hue.
III.
And when the spring comes with her host
Of flowers, that flower beloved the most
Shrinks from the crowd that may confuse
Her heavenly odour and virgin hues.
IV.
Pluck the others, but still remember
Their herald out of dim December —
The morning star of all the flowers,
The pledge of daylight's lengthened hours;20
Nor, midst the roses, e'er forget
The virgin — virgin Violet.

[529]
Enter CÆSAR.
Cæs. (singing).
The wars are all over,
Our swords are all idle,
The steed bites the bridle,
The casque's on the wall.
There's rest for the rover;
But his armour is rusty,
And the veteran grows crusty,
As he yawns in the hall.30
He drinks—but what's drinking?
A mere pause from thinking!
No bugle awakes him with life-and-death call.
Chorus.
But the hound bayeth loudly,
The boar's in the wood,
And the falcon longs proudly
To spring from her hood:
On the wrist of the noble
She sits like a crest,
And the air is in trouble40
With birds from their nest.
Cæs.
Oh! shadow of Glory!
Dim image of War!
But the chase hath no story,
Her hero no star,
Since Nimrod, the founder
Of empire and chase,
Who made the woods wonder
And quake for their race.
When the lion was young,50
In the pride of his might,
Then 'twas sport for the strong

To embrace him in fight;
To go forth, with a pine
For a spear, 'gainst the mammoth,
Or strike through the ravine[du]
At the foaming behemoth;[530]
While man was in stature
As towers in our time,
The first born of Nature,60
And, like her, sublime!
Chorus.
But the wars are over,
The spring is come;
The bride and her lover
Have sought their home:
They are happy, and we rejoice;
Let their hearts have an echo from every voice!
 [Exeunt the Peasantry, singing.

[531]

# FRAGMENT OF THE THIRD PART OF THE DEFORMED TRANSFORMED.

Chorus.
When the merry bells are ringing,
And the peasant girls are singing,
And the early flowers are flinging
Their odours in the air;
And the honey bee is clinging
To the buds; and birds are winging
Their way, pair by pair:
Then the earth looks free from trouble
With the brightness of a bubble:
Though I did not make it,10
I could breathe on and break it;
But too much I scorn it,
Or else I would mourn it,
To see despots and slaves
Playing o'er their own graves.
Enter COUNT ARNOLD.

Mem. Jealous—Arnold of Cæsar.
Olympia at first not liking Cæsar
—then?—Arnold jealous of himself
under his former figure, owing to
the power of intellect, etc., etc., etc.
Arnold. You are merry, Sir—what? singing too?
Cæsar.It is
The land of Song—and Canticles you know
Were once my avocation.
Arn.Nothing moves you;
You scoff even at your own calamity[532]—

And such calamity! how wert thou fallen20
Son of the Morning! and yet Lucifer
Can smile.
Cæs.His shape can—would you have me weep,
In the fair form I wear, to please you?
Arn.Ah!
Cæs. You are grave—what have you on your spirit!
Arn.Nothing.
Cæs. How mortals lie by instinct! If you ask
A disappointed courtier—What's the matter?
"Nothing"—an outshone Beauty what has made
Her smooth brow crisp—"Oh, Nothing!"—a young heir
When his Sire has recovered from the Gout,
What ails him? "Nothing!" or a Monarch who30
Has heard the truth, and looks imperial on it—
What clouds his royal aspect? "Nothing," "Nothing!"
Nothing—eternal nothing—of these nothings
All are a lie—for all to them are much!
And they themselves alone the real "Nothings."
Your present Nothing, too, is something to you—
What is it?
Arn.Know you not?
Cæs.I only know
What I desire to know! and will not waste
Omniscience upon phantoms. Out with it!
If you seek aid from me—or else be silent.40
And eat your thoughts—till they breed snakes within you.
Arn. Olimpia!
Cæs.I thought as much—go on.
Arn. I thought she had loved me.
Cæs.Blessings on your Creed!
What a good Christian you were found to be!
But what cold Sceptic hath appalled your faith
And transubstantiated to crumbs again
The body of your Credence?

Arn.No one—but—
Each day—each hour—each minute shows me more
And more she loves me not—
Cæs.Doth she rebel?
Arn. No, she is calm, and meek, and silent with me,50
And coldly dutiful, and proudly patient—[533]
Endures my Love—not meets it.
Cæs.That seems strange.
You are beautiful and brave! the first is much
For passion—and the rest for Vanity.
Arn. I saved her life, too; and her Father's life,
And Father's house from ashes.
Cæs.These are nothing.
You seek for Gratitude—the Philosopher's stone.
Arn. And find it not.
Cæs.You cannot find what is not.
But found would it content you? would you owe
To thankfulness what you desire from Passion?60
No! No! you would be loved—what you call loved—
Self-loved—loved for yourself—for neither health,
Nor wealth, nor youth, nor power, nor rank, nor beauty—
For these you may be stript of—but beloved
As an abstraction—for—you know not what!
These are the wishes of a moderate lover—
And so you love.
Arn.Ah! could I be beloved,
Would I ask wherefore?
Cæs.Yes! and not believe
The answer—You are jealous.
Arn.And of whom?
Cæs. It may be of yourself,[252] for Jealousy70
Is as a shadow of the Sun. The Orb
Is mighty—as you mortals deem—and to
Your little Universe seems universal;
But, great as He appears, and is to you,

The smallest cloud—the slightest vapour of
Your humid earth enables you to look
Upon a Sky which you revile as dull;
Though your eyes dare not gaze on it when cloudless.
Nothing can blind a mortal like to light.
Now Love in you is as the Sun—a thing80
Beyond you—and your Jealousy's of Earth[534]—
A cloud of your own raising.
Arn.Not so always!
There is a cause at times.
Cæs.Oh, yes! when atoms jostle,
The System is in peril. But I speak
Of things you know not. Well, to earth again!
This precious thing of dust—this bright Olimpia—
This marvellous Virgin, is a marble maid—
An Idol, but a cold one to your heat
Promethean, and unkindled by your torch.
Arn. Slave!
Cæs.In the victor's Chariot, when Rome triumphed,90
There was a Slave of yore to tell him truth!
You are a Conqueror—command your Slave.
Arn. Teach me the way to win the woman's love.
Cæs. Leave her.
Arn.Where that the path—I'd not pursue it.
Cæs. No doubt! for if you did, the remedy
Would be for a disease already cured.
Arn. All wretched as I am, I would not quit
My unrequited love, for all that's happy.
Cæs. You have possessed the woman—still possess.
What need you more?
Arn.To be myself possessed—100
To be her heart as she is mine.

# FOOTNOTES

[201][The Three Brothers, by Joshua Pickersgill, junior, was published in 1803. There is no copy of The Three Brothers in the British Museum. The following extracts are taken from a copy in the Bodleian Library at Oxford (vol. 4, cap. xi. pp. 229-350): —

"Arnaud, the natural son of the Marquis de Souvricour, was a child 'extraordinary in Beauty and Intellect.' When travelling with his parents to Languedoc, Arnaud being 8 years old, he was shot at by banditti, and forsaken by his parents. The Captain of the band nursed him. 'But those perfections to which Arnaud owed his existence, ceased to adorn it. The ball had gored his shoulder, and the fall had dislocated it; by the latter misadventure his spine likewise was so fatally injured as to be irrecoverable to its pristine uprightness. Injuries so compound confounded the Captain, who sorrowed to see a creature so charming, at once deformed by a crooked back and an excrescent shoulder.' Arnaud was found and taken back to his parents. 'The bitterest consciousness of his deformity was derived from their indelicate, though, perhaps, insensible alteration of conduct.... Of his person he continued to speak as of an abhorrent enemy.... "Were a blessing submitted to my choice, I would say, [said Arnaud] be it my immediate dissolution." "I think," said his mother, ... "that you could wish better." "Yes," adjoined Arnaud, "for that wish should be that I ever had remained unborn."' He polishes the broken blade of a sword, and views himself therein; the sight so horrifies him that he determines to throw himself over a precipice, but draws back at the last moment. He goes to a cavern, and conjures up the prince of hell. "Arnaud knew himself to be interrogated. What he required.... What was that answer the effects explain.... There passed in liveliest portraiture the various men distinguished for that beauty and grace which Arnaud so much desired, that he was ambitious to purchase them with his soul. He felt that it was his part to chuse whom he would resemble, yet he remained unresolved, though the spectator of an hundred shades of renown, among which glided by Alexander, Alcibiades, and Hephestion: at length appeared the supernatural effigy of a man, whose perfections human artist never could depict or insculp—Demetrius, the son of Antigonus. Arnaud's heart heaved quick with preference, and strait he found within his hand the resemblance of a poniard, its point inverted towards his breast. A mere automaton in the hands of the Demon, he thrust the point through his heart, and underwent a painless death. During his trance, his spirit metempsychosed from the body of his detestation to that of his admiration ... Arnaud awoke a Julian!'"]

[202][For a résumé of M. G. Lewis's Wood Demon (afterwards re-cast as One O'clock; or, The Knight and the Wood-Demon, 1811), see "First Visit to the Theatre in London," Poems, by Hartley Coleridge, 1851, i., Appendix C, pp. cxcix.-cciii. The Wood Demon in its original form was never published.]

[203][Mrs. Shelley inscribed the following note on the fly-leaf of her copy of The Deformed Transformed:—

"This had long been a favourite subject with Lord Byron. I think that he mentioned it also in Switzerland. I copied it—he sending a portion of it at a time, as it was finished, to me. At this time he had a great horror of its being said that he plagiarised, or that he studied for ideas, and wrote with difficulty. Thus he gave Shelley Aikins' edition of the British poets, that it might not be found in his house by some English lounger, and reported home; thus, too, he always dated when he began and when he ended a poem, to prove hereafter how quickly it was done. I do not think that he altered a line in this drama after he had once written it down. He composed and corrected in his mind. I do not know how he meant to finish it; but he said himself that the whole conduct of the story was already conceived. It was at this time that a brutal paragraph[*] alluding to his lameness appeared, which he repeated to me lest I should hear it from some one else. No action of Lord Byron's life—scarce a line he has written—but was influenced by his personal defect."]

[[*] It is possible that Mrs. Shelley alludes to a sentence in the Memoirs, etc., of Lord Byron. (by Dr. John Watkin), 1822, p. 46: "A malformation of one of his feet, and other indications of a rickety constitution, served as a plea for suffering him to range the hills and to wander about at his pleasure on the seashore, that his frame might be invigorated by air and exercise."]

[cv] The Deformed—a drama.—B. Pisa, 1822.

[204][Moore (Life, p. 13) quotes these lines in connection with a passage in Byron's "Memoranda," where, in speaking of his own sensitiveness on the subject of his deformed foot, he described the feeling of horror and humiliation that came over him, when his mother, in one of her fits of passion, called him "a lame brat!"... "It may be questioned," he adds, "whether that whole drama [The Deformed Transformed] was not indebted for its origin to that single recollection."

Byron's early letters (e.g. November 2, 11, 17, 1804, Letters, 1898, i. 41, 45, 48) are full of complaints of his mother's "eccentric behaviour," her "fits of phrenzy," her "caprices," "passions," and so forth; and there is convincing proof—see Life, pp. 28, 306; Letters, 1898, ii. 122 (incident at Bellingham's execution); Letters, 1901, vi. 179 (Le Diable Boiteux)—that he regarded the contraction of the muscles of his legs as a more or less repulsive deformity. And yet, to quote one of a hundred testimonies,—"with regard to Lord Byron's features, Mr. Mathews observed, that he was the only man he ever contemplated, to whom he felt disposed to apply the word beautiful" (Memoirs of Charles Matthews, 1838, ii. 380). The looker-on or the consoler computes the magnitude and the liberality of the compensation. The sufferer thinks only of his sufferings.]

[205][So, too, Prospero to Caliban, Tempest, act i. sc. 2, line 309, etc.]

[206][Compare—"Have not partook oppression." Marino Faliero, act i. sc. 2, line 468, Poetical Works, 1901, iv. 362, note 1.]

[207][Compare the story of the philosopher Jamblichus and the raising of Eros and Anteros from their "fountain-dwellings."—Manfred, act ii. sc. 2, line 93, Poetical Works, 1901, iv. 105, note 2.]

[cw] Give me the strength of the buffalo's foot (which marks me).—[MS.]

[cx]The sailless dromedary— —.—[MS.]

[cy] Now I can gibe the mightiest.—[MS.]

[208][So, too, in The Tragical History of Dr. Faustus (Marlowe's Works, 1858, p. 112), Faustus stabs his arm, "and with his proper blood Assures his soul to be great Lucifer's."]

[cz]
Walk lively and pliant.
You shall rise up as pliant.—[MS, erased.]

[209]This is a well-known German superstition—a gigantic shadow produced by reflection on the Brocken. [See Brewster's Letters on Natural Magic, 1831, p. 128.]

[da]And such my command.—[MS.]

[210]["Nigris vegetisque oculis."—Suetonius, Vitæ C. Julius Cæsar, cap. xiv., Opera Omnia, 1826, i. 105.]

[211][Vide post, p. 501, note 1.]

[212]["Sed ante alias [Julius Cæsar] dilexit M. Bruti matrem Serviliam ... dilexit et reginas ... sed maxime Cleopatram" (ibid., i. 113, 115). Cleopatra, born B.C. 69, was twenty-one years old when she met Cæsar, B.C. 48.]

[db]
And can
It be? the man who shook the earth is gone.—[MS.]

[213]["Upon the whole, it may be doubted whether there be a name of Antiquity which comes down with such a general

charm as that of Alcibiades. Why? I cannot answer: who can?"—Detached Thoughts (1821), No. 108, Letters, 1901, v. 461. For Sir Walter Scott's note on this passage, see Letters, 1900, iv. 77, 78, note 2.]

[214][The outside of Socrates was that of a satyr and buffoon, but his soul was all virtue, and from within him came such divine and pathetic things, as pierced the heart, and drew tears from the hearers.—Plato, Symp., p. 216, D.]

[215]["Anthony had a noble dignity of countenance, a graceful length of beard, a large forehead, an aquiline nose: and, upon the whole, the same manly aspect that we see in the pictures and statues of Hercules."—Plutarch's Lives, Langhorne's Translation, 1838, p. 634.]

[216][As in the "Farnese" Hercules.]

[217][The beauty and mien [of Demetrius Poliorcetes] were so inimitable that no statuary or painter could hit off a likeness. His countenance had a mixture of grace and dignity; and was at once amiable and awful; and the unsubdued and eager air of youth was blended with the majesty of the hero and the king.—Plutarch's Lives, Langhorne's Translation, 1838, p. 616. Demetrius the Besieger rescued Greece from the sway of Ptolemy and Cassander, B.C. 307. He passed the following winter at Athens, where divine honours were paid to him under the title of "the Preserver" (ὁ Σωτήρ). He was "the shame of Greece in peace," by reason of his profligacy—"the citadel was so polluted with his debaucheries, that it appeared to be kept sacred in some degree when he indulged himself only with such Hetæræ as Chrysis, Lamia, Demo, and Anticyra." He was the unspiritual ancestor of Charles the Second. Once when his father, Antigonus, had been told that he was indisposed, "he went to see him; and when he came to the door, he met one of his favourites going out. He went in, however, and, sitting down by him, took hold of his hand. 'My fever,' said Demetrius, 'has left me.' 'I knew it,' said

Antigonus, 'for I met it this moment at the door.'" — Plutarch's
Lives, ibid., pp. 621-623.]

[218][Spercheus was a river-god, the husband of Polydora, the
daughter of Peleus. Peleus casts into the river the hair of his
son Achilles, in the pious hope that his son-in-law would
accept the votive offering, and grant the youth a safe return
from the Trojan war. See Iliad, xxiii. 140, sqq.]

[219]["Whosoever," says Bacon, "hath anything fixed in his
person that doth induce contempt, hath also a perpetual spur
in himself to rescue and deliver himself from scorn; therefore,
all deformed persons are extreme bold; first, as in their own
defence, as being exposed to scorn, but in process of time by a
general habit; also it stirreth in them industry, and especially
of this kind, to watch and observe the weakness of others, that
they may have somewhat to repay." (Essay xliv.). Byron's
"chief incentive, when a boy, to distinction was that mark of
deformity on his person, by an acute sense of which he was
first stung into the ambition of being great."— Life, p. 306.]

[220][Timúr Bey, or Timúr Lang, i.e. "the lame Timúr" (A.D.
1336-1405), was the founder of the Mogul dynasty. He was the
Tamerlane of history and of legend. Byron had certainly read
the selections from Marlowe's Tamburlaine the Great, in
Lamb's Specimens of English Dramatic Poets.]

[221]["I am black, but comely."— Song of Solomon i. 5.]

[222]Adam means "red earth," from which the first man was
formed. [The word adām is said to be analogous to the
Assyrian admu, "child"— i.e. "one made" by God. — Encycl.
Bibl., art. "Adam."]

[dc] This shape into Life. — [MS.]

[223][The reference is to the homunculi of the alchymists. See
Retzsch's illustrations to Goethe's Faust, 1834, plates 3, 4, 5.
Compare, too, The Second Part of Faust, act ii. —

"The glass rings low, the charming power that lives
Within it makes the music that it gives.
It dims! it brightens! it will shape itself.

And see! a graceful dazzling little elf.
He lives! he moves! spruce mannikin of fire,
What more can we? what more can earth desire?"
Anster's Translation, 1886, p. 91.]
[dd]Your Interloper — —.—[MS.]
[224][Compare Prisoner of Chillon, stanza ii. line 35, Poetical
Works, 1091, iv. 15, note i. Compare, too, the dialogue
between Mephistopheles and the Will-o'-the Wisp, in the
scene on the Hartz Mountains, in Faust, Part I. (see Anster's
Translation, 1886, p. 271).]
[225][The immediate reference is to the composite forces,
German, French, and Spanish, of the Imperial Army under the
command of Charles de Bourbon: but there is in lines 498-507
a manifest allusion to the revolutionary movements in South
America, Italy, and Spain, which were at their height in 1822.
(See the Age of Bronze, section vi. lines 260, sq., post, pp. 555-
557.)]
[226][See Euripides, Hippolytus, line 733.]
[de]Kochlani — —.—[MS.]
[227][Kochlani horses were bred in a central province of
Arabia.]
[228][Byron's knowledge of Huon of Bordeaux was, most
probably, derived from Sotheby's Oberon; or, Huon de
Bourdeux: A Mask, published in 1802. For The Boke of Duke
Huon of Burdeux, done into English by Sir John Bourchier,
Lord Berners, see the reprint issued by the Early English Text
Society (E.S., No. xliii. 1884); and for Analyse de Huon de
Bordeaux, etc., see Les Epopées Françaises, by Léon Gautier,
1880, ii. 719-773.]
[229][The so-called statue of Memnon, the beautiful son of
Tithonus and Eos (Dawn), is now known to be that of
Amenhotep III., who reigned in the eighteenth dynasty, about
1430 B.C. Strabo, ed. 1807. p. 1155, was the first to record the
musical note which sounded from the statue when it was
touched by the rays of the rising sun. It used to be argued (see

Gifford's note to Don Juan, Canto XIII. stanza lxiv. line 3, ed. 1837, p. 731) that the sounds were produced by a trick, but of late years it has been maintained that the Memnon's wail was due to natural causes, the pressure of suddenly-warmed currents of air through the pores and crevices of the stone. After the statue was restored, the phenomenon ceased. (See La statue vocale de Memnon, par J. A. Letronne, Paris, 1833, pp. 55, 56.)]

[df]We'll add a "Count" to it. — [MS.]

[dg] — — my eyes are full. — [MS.]

[230][Charles de Bourbon, Comte de Montpensier et de la Marche, Dauphin d'Auvergne, was born February 17, 1490. He served in Italy with Bayard, and helped to decide the victory of Agnadello (A.D. 1510). He was appointed Constable of France by Francis I., January, 1515, and fought at the battle of Marignano, September 13, 1515. Not long afterwards he lost the king's favour, who was set against him by his mother, Louise de Savoie; was recalled from his command in Italy, and superseded by Odet de Foix, brother of the king's mistress. It was not, however, till he became a widower (Susanne, Duchesse de Bourbon, died April 28, 1521) that he finally broke with Francis and attached himself to the Emperor Charles V. Madame, the king's mother, not only coveted the vast estates of the house of Bourbon, but was enamoured of the Constable's person, and, so to speak, gave him his choice between marriage and a suit for his fiefs. Charles would have nothing to say to the lady's proposals or to her son's entreaties, and seeing that rejection meant ruin, he "entered into a correspondence with the Emperor and the King [Henry VIII.] of England ... and, finding this discovered, went into the Emperor's service."

After various and varying successes, both in the South of France and in Lombardy, he found himself, in the spring of 1527, not so much the commander-in-chief as the popular capo of a mixed body of German, Spanish, and Italian condottieri, unpaid and ill-disciplined, who had mutinied more than once, who could only be kept together by the prospect of unlimited booty, and a timely concession to their demands. "To Rome! to Rome!" cried the hungry and tumultuous landsknechts, and on May 5, 1527, the "late Constable of France," at the head of an army of 30,000 troops, appeared before the walls of the sacred city. On the morning of the 6th of May, he was killed by a shot from an arquebuse. His epitaph recounts his honours: "Aucto Imperio, Gallo victo, Superatâ Italiâ, Pontifice obsesso, Româ captâ, Borbonius, Hic Jacet;" but in Paris they painted the sill of his gate-way yellow, because he was a renegade and a traitor. He could not have said, with the dying Bayard, "Ne me plaignez pas-je meurs sans avoir servi contre ma patrie, mon roy, et mon serment." (See Modern Universal History, 1760, xxiv. 150-152, Note C; Nouvelle Biographie Universelle, art. "Bourbon.")]

[231][The contrast is between imperial Rome, the Lord of the world, and papal Rome, "the great harlot which hath corrupted the earth with her fornications" (Rev. ii. 19). Compare Part II. sc. iii. line 26, vide post, p. 521.]

[232][Compare Manfred, act iii. sc. 4, line 10; and Childe Harold, Canto IV. stanza cxxviii. line 1; Poetical Works, 1901, iv. 131, 1899, ii. 423, note 2.]

[233]["Calvitii vero deformitatem iniquissime ferret, sæpe obtrectatorum jocis obnoxiam expertus. Ideoque et deficientem capillum revocare a vertice assuerat, et ex omnibus decretis sibi a Senatu populoque honoribus non aliud aut recepit aut usurpavit libentius, quam jus laureæ coronæ perpetuo gestandæ."—Suetonius, Opera Omnia, 1826, pp. 105, 106.]

[234][Francis the First was taken prisoner at the Battle of Pavia, February 24, 1525.]

[dh]With a soldier's firm foot.—[MS.]

[235][Compare The Siege of Corinth, line 752, Poetical Works, 1900, iii. 483. There is a note of tragic irony in the soldiers' vain-glorious prophecy.]

[di]With the Bourbon will count o'er. — [MS.]

[236][Brantôme (Memoires, etc., 1722, i. 215) quotes a "chanson" of "Les soldats Espagnols" as they marched Romewards. "Calla calla Julio Cesar, Hannibal, y Scipion! Viva la fama de Bourbon."]

[dj]The General with his men of confidence. — [MS.]

[dk] And present phantom of that deathless world. — [MS.]

[237][When the Uticans decided not to stand a siege, but to send deputies to Cæsar, Cato determined to put an end to his life rather than fall into the hands of the conqueror. Accordingly, after he had retired to rest he stabbed himself under the breast, and when the physician sewed up the wound, he thrust him away, and plucked out his own bowels. — Plutarch's Lives, Langhorne's Translation, 1838, P. 553.]

[dl] Of a mere starving— —. — [MS.]

[dm] — —Work away with words. — [MS.]

[dn] First City rests upon to-morrow's action. — [MS.]

[238]["Dès l'aube du lundi 6 mai 1527, le connétable, à cheval, la cuirasse couverte d'un manteau blanc, marcha vers le Borgo, dont les murailles, à la hauteur de San-Spirito, étaient d'accès facile.... Bourbon mit pied à terre, et, prenant lui-même une échelle l'appliqua tout près de la porte Torrione." — De l'Italie, par Émile Gebhart, 1876, p. 255. Cæsar Grolierius (Historia expugnatæ ... Urbis, 1637), who claims to speak as an eye-witness (p. 2), describes "Borbonius" as "insignemque veste et armis" (p. 62).]

[do]'Tis the morning — Hark! Hark! Hark! — [MS.]

[239] Scipio, the second Africanus, is said to have repeated a verse of Homer [Iliad, vi. 448], and wept over the burning of Carthage [B.C. 146]. He had better have granted it a capitulation.

[dp]Than such victors should pollute.—[MS.]

[240][Byron retains or adopts the old-fashioned pronunciation of the word "Rome" metri gratiâ. Compare The Island, Canto II. line 199.]

[241]["Le bouillant Bourbon, à la tête des plus intrepides assaillans tenoit, de la main gauche une échelle appuyée centre le mur, et de la droite faisoit signe à ses soldats de monter pour suivre leurs camarades; en ce moment il reçut dans le flanc une balle d'arquebuse qui le traversa de part en part; il tomba à terre, mortellement blessé. On rapporte qu'avant d'expirer il prononca ces mots: 'Officiers et soldats, cacher ma mort à l'ennemi et marchez toujours en avant; la victoire est à vous, mon trépas ne peut vous la ravir.'"—Sac de Rome en 1527, par Jacques Buonaparte, 1836, p. 201.]

[242]["Quand il sentit le coup, se print à cryer: 'Jésus!' et puis il dist 'Hélas! mon Dieu, je suis mort!' Si prit son espée par la poignée en signe de croix en disant tout hault, 'Miserere mei, Deus, secundùm magnam misericordiam tuam.'"—Chronique de Bayart, 1836, cap. lxiv., p. 119. For his rebuke of Charles de Bourbon, "Ne me plaignez pas," etc., vide ante, p. 499.]

[243]["'M. de Bourbon,' dit un contemporain, 'termina de vie par mort, mais avant fist le devoir de bon, Chrestien; car il se confessa et reçut son Créateur.'"—De l'Italie, par Émile Gebhart, 1876, p. 256.]

[244]["While I was at work upon that diabolical task of mine, there came, from time to time, to watch me, some of the Cardinals who were invested in the castle; and most frequently the Cardinal of Ravenna and the Cardinal de' Gaddi. I often told them not to show themselves, since their nasty red caps gave a fair mark for the enemy." —Life of Benvenuto Cellini, translated by J. A. Symonds, 1888, i. 112. See, too, for the flight of the Cardinals, Sac de Rome, par Jacques Buonaparte, Paris, 1836, p. 203.]

[dq] Covered with gore and glory—those good times.—[MS.]

[245]["Directing my arquebuse where I saw the thickest and most serried troop of fighting men, I aimed exactly at one whom I remarked to be higher than the rest; the fog prevented me from being certain whether he was on horseback or on foot. Then I turned to Alessandro and Cecchino, and bade them discharge their arquebuses, showing them how to avoid being hit by the besiegers. When we had fired two rounds apiece, I crept cautiously up to the walls, and observing a most extraordinary confusion, I discovered afterwards that one of our shots had killed the Constable of Bourbon; and from what I subsequently learned he was the man whom I had first noticed above the heads of the rest." It is a fact "that Bourbon was shot dead near the spot Cellini mentions. But the honour of flying the arquebuse ... cannot be assigned to any one in particular."—Life of Benvenuto Cellini, 1888, i. 114, and note.]

[246][Compare Ode to Napoleon Buonaparte, stanza vi. line 2, Poetical Works, 1900, in. 307, note 3.]

[dr]

'Tis the moment
When such I fain would show me.—[MS.]

[247][Among the Imperial troops which Charles de Bourbon led against Rome were at least six thousand Landsknechts, ardent converts to the Reformed religion, and eager to prove their zeal by the slaughter of Catholics and the destruction of altars and crucifixes. Their leader, George Frundsberg, had set out for Rome with the pious intention of hanging the Pope (see The Popes of Rome, by Leopold Ranke, translated by Sarah Austen, 1866, i. 72). Brantôme (Memoirs de Messire Pierre de Bourdeille.... Leyde, 1722, i. 230) gives a vivid picture of their fanatical savagery: "Leur cruauté ne s'estendit pas seulement sur les personnes, mais sur les marbres et les anciennes statuës. Les Lansquenets, qui nouvellement estoient imbus de la nouvelle Religion, et les Espagnols encore aussi bien que les autres, s'habilloient en Cardinaux et evesques en

leur habits Pontificaux et se pourmenoient ainsi parray la Ville."

In the Schmalkald articles, 1530, the pious belief that the Pope was Antichrist became an article of the Lutheran creed. Compare the following extracts, quoted by Hans Schultz in Der Sacco di Roma, 1894, p. 63, from the Historia von der Romischen Bischoff, etc., 1527:

"Der Papst ist für den Verfasser der Antichrist, der durch Lug und Trug seine Herrschaft in der Welt behauptet."

"Quant à l'armée impériale, on n'en vit jamais de plus étonnante…. Allemands et Espagnols, luthériens iconoclastes qui brûlaient les églises, ou furieux mystiques qui brûlaient Juils et Maures, barbares plus raffinés que leur vieux ancêtres les Visigoths, les Vandales et les Huns, ils frappaient l'Italie d'une terreur sans exemple."—De I'italie, by E. Gebliart, chap. vii., "Le Sac de Rome en 1527," p. 245.]

[ds]

Hush! don't let him hear you
Or he might take you off before your time.—[MS.]

[248]["We got with the greatest difficulty to the gate of the castle…. I ascended to the keep, and, at the same instant, Pope Clement came in through the corridors into the castle; he had refused to leave the palace of St. Peter earlier, being unable to believe that his enemies would effect their entrance into Rome."—Life of Benvenuto Cellini, translated by J. A. Symonds, 1888, i. 114, 115.

So, too, Jacques Buonaparte (Le Sac de Rome, 1836, p. 202): "Le Pape Clement, avoit entendu les cris des soldats; il se sauvoit précipitamment par un long corridor pratiqué dans un mur double et se laissoit emporter de son palais an château Saint-Ange."]

[249][Penthesilea, Queen of the Amazons, was slain by Achilles, who wept over her as she lay a-dying, bewailing her beauty and her daring. For the picture, see Pausanias, Descriptio Græciæ, lib, v. cap. 11, 2.]

[250][See Gen. vi. 2, the motto of Heaven and Earth, ante, p, 277.]

[251]["It came to pass the same day, that in Echatane a city of Media, Sara the daughter of Raguel was also reproached by her father's maids; because that she had been married to seven husbands, whom Asmodeus the evil spirit had killed before they had lain with her.... And as he went, he remembered the words of Raphael, and took the ashes of the perfumes, and put the heart and the liver of the fish thereupon, and made smoke therewith. The which smell when the evil spirit had smelled, he fled into the utmost parts of Egypt." — Tobit iii. 7, 8; viii. 2, 3.]

[dt] The first born who burst the winter sun. — [MS.]

[du] — — through the brine. — [MS.]

[252][Lucifer or Mephistopheles, renamed Cæsar, wears the shape of the Deformed Arnold. It may be that Byron intended to make Olimpia bestow her affections, not on the glorious Achilles, but the witty and interesting Hunchback.]

Made in the USA
Columbia, SC
30 December 2017